Building a culture for understanding, acceptance, and change.

"So THAT's why you're like that!"

By
Tod Faller

"Others will begin treating you differently, more positively, and *they* won't even know why they're doing it...guaranteed!"

Cartoons by Brian Faller

"So THAT'S WHY YOU'RE LIKE THAT!"

By

Tod Faller

copyright ©2005 Tod Faller

All rights reserved. No part of this publication may be reproduced or transmitted in any other form or for any means, electronic or mechanical, including photocopy, recording or any information storage system, without written permission from Headline Books, Inc.

To order additional copies of this book or for book publishing information, or to contact the author:

Headline Books & Co.
P.O. Box 52
Terra Alta, WV 26764
www.headlinebooks.com

Tel/Fax: 800-570-5951 or 304-789-3001
Email: tod@todfaller.com
www.todfaller.com

ISBN 0929915372

Library of Congress Control Number: 2005933492

PRINTED IN THE UNITED STATES OF AMERICA

Dedication

*For Irene, my "Teacher Down the Hall,"
. . . and to all those who work in the
trenches of education:
Our Teachers and Principals.*

...and for my grandbabies

Table of Contents

Foreword 5

Introduction
NCLB: Negative Choices (are)
Learned Behaviors 7

Chapter 1
Understanding the Nature of Behavior:
Eight Wonders of the World 11

Chapter 2
How to Spoil Your Child and Raise an
Irresponsible Adult 26

Chapter 3
All Behaviors are Learned:
The Games People Play 31

Chapter 4
All Behaviors are Choices:
Happiness is Optional 54

Chapter 5
All Behaviors can Change:
The Application of Understanding 71

Forward

Education and "The Funnel Theory"

The System:
In the world of state and national Public Education, there is a pipeline that connects "what is expected" with "who is expected to do it." This is the conduit that connects those who are responsible for directing public education…from those who will be held accountable for it. For many in the trenches of education, the teachers and principals, it is simply referred to as "The Funnel."

At the federal, state and district level, teachers envision a literal army of clerks, staffers, attorneys, legislators, coordinators, supervisors, specialist, assistants, and program directors gathered around this huge funnel in the sky. These are the faceless masses responsible for dropping the endless array of legislation, mandates, directives, assessments, surveys, checklists, regulations, interpretations, certifications, evaluations, initiative, training requirements, programs, and policies on the overflowing desk of every school level educator. On top of that pile will fall the array of reform initiatives, revisions, and updates that will inevitably follow down the funnel.

Every one of the hundreds of departments, and the tens of thousands of detached individuals in the educational system, exist only to serve the funnel. Countless departments, each with their own agendas, timelines and sets of expectations for principals and teachers, jockey for position around the funnel. Having carved yet another new initiative, each proud participant drops his/her assorted directives and mandates down the funnel before scurrying back to separate offices to create the predictable corrections and updates. While hundreds of independent souls from countless agencies, departments and organizations drop their contents into the mouth of the funnel—it will inevitably fall on the same two desks—the principal's desk and the teacher's desk.

Since 2001, the compulsion to pack "the funnel" comes from the 21st century accountability in education legislation known as No Child Left Behind (NCLB). While purposeful in its intent, there appears to be no reins on this horse. The premise seems to be, keep dropping expectations and mandates down the funnel and surely student learning, social behavior, maturity, responsibility, character development and appropriate attire will improve. To encourage compliance and to raise the morale of those sagging under the considerable weight of these expectations, school level educators have been offered sanctions, threats, intimidation, greater demands and less time to fulfill it all. The growing image of "more bricks with less straw" comes to mind. The funnel never stops.

There are apparently only three rules to be considered before the funnel can be accessed by its users. First, judging by the number of contradictions and corrections that clog the funnel, you are apparently not permitted to collaborate with other departments or agencies before dropping memos, mandates, and expectations down this chute. Second, you must force yourself to believe…among the *hundreds* of federal, state, and local agencies, departments and organizations that are daily users of the funnel…that *you alone* are requiring every principal and teacher to immediately read, distribute, implement, provide subsequent training, and meet your deadlines. Third, you must be completely detached from reality.

The Reality:

Consider the vast sea of insecure, hyper, excited, nervous, prepubescent adolescents that transform silent school buildings at 7 a.m. every morning, into loud, overcrowded classrooms, corridors, and gymnasiums by 7:30. The school day is consumed with activity. Literally every minute of the teacher's time is scheduled with instruction, supervision of children, meetings, conferences, or planning. Accountability is what drives all instruction. Educators are being held accountable for far more than the teaching of academics, but are being increasingly reminded that they will be held personally responsible if specific academic levels… standards and norms determined by those who fill the funnel… are not met.

Students leave at the end of the school day, many returning to empty homes and to unlimited Internet access. Most are subject to sexually explicit television programming that began long before they got home, will run through "prime time," and continue long after they were supposed to have drifted off to sleep. Every child's overpowering human need is for peer acceptance. They pull out those cell phones before their butts hit the bus seats and can't wait to reconnect later with their classmates on the telephone or online. The next morning, many without the benefit of breakfast, will board the same bus again and will carry back to their classmates, everything that was said, implied, offered, or threatened the night before. They will meet to act out their fears, insecurities and excitement in the only place they will come together all week—in school. The teachers have prepared plans for the day…so have their students.

Enter into our schools and lives—CONFLICT

Introduction

NCLB: Negative Choices (are) Learned Behaviors

"Violence is the voice of the unheard."

—Martin Luther King

CONFLICT is not the same as VIOLENCE. While the two get the same play on the nightly news, conflict is a daily way of life. Internal conflict exists in the frustration of catching every red light on your way to work, in replaying what you "should have said" to that angry parent, and in smiling at co-workers when you would rather kick them in the shins. While conflict is common, actual violence, thank God, is rare.

While there are violent and traumatic incidents in our nation's schools, how many can you point to as being spontaneous acts of aggression? While these acts were explosive moments, they were instead acts of premeditated aggression that often were planned, undetected, and boiling beneath the surface for some time prior to the incident. *"There were signs that this was going to happen,"* the bystanders always seem to say, but this comes long after the fact.

Do we simply not understand the signs? Could it be that conflict is just uncomfortable and, therefore, better left ignored? Perhaps that way, it will just go away? Maybe it is because we simply do not *understand and accept* that unresolved internal conflict or "silent rage" will lead to violence? Maybe we don't realize how we can help ourselves... or others... to better understand and accept the nature of human behavior. Maybe we can't see the difference between our *behavior* and our *needs*.

The first book in "The Teacher Down the Hall" Seminar Series, was entitled, *"What did you do THAT for?"* The answer to that question... and the resolution to conflict... comes with the understanding that all human behaviors serve only to satisfy one of five basic human needs: Survival; Love and Acceptance; Affirmation and Fulfillment; Fun; and Freedom.

We constantly are choosing behaviors to get us what we want because what we are always after is some of what we need. When others won't give us what we want... conflict is born. We struggle with our internal thoughts and say, *"What am I to do now to get what I want?"*

This internal struggle, this mental tug-of-war of voices being played out inside your head, is referred to as *Intra*personal Conflict. Only if you are willing to look past the behaviors of others, to see the particular needs others are trying to satisfy with their choice of behaviors, will you *know* the internal peace that comes with such understanding and acceptance. As all behaviors are attempts to meet one or more of only five basic needs, the person who first chooses to work to meet these needs in others, has moved past understanding towards acceptance.

When we disagree with those who say *"NO, you can't have this thing you want,"* we will *always* make one of two choices: we will *either accept* "NO" for an answer, even if we don't agree, or we will escalate our behaviors in an attempt to control the person who told us "No" into saying "Yes." If you choose *not* to accept, you will select behaviors that you believe will control that person who told you "No" to change his/her mind. This is the beginning of *Inter*personal Conflict as we have now taken our *intra*personal thoughts and turned them into outward behaviors in opposition to the will of others. The *Intra*personal conflict we will continue to experience, and the interpersonal conflict that will begin as a direct result of our internal decisions to exercise controlling behaviors, is played out hundreds and hundreds of times a day...*every single day.* This is the nature of our human nature (Chapter 1).

"So THAT'S why you're like that!" is the follow up to book one in *"The Teacher Down The Hall Seminar Series."* This book, *"What did you do THAT for?"* expands the readers understanding of behaviors and needs presented in book one by providing relevant stories and examples of humans in and out of relationships. Our success in life, our happiness, is tied to the relationships we build and hold with others. When it comes to the importance of teaching and building relationships with children (and families), Dr. Ruby Payne, in her work and research in generational poverty affirms, *"Relationships are the key to motivating children to learn."* The extent to which we are able to build long standing relationships is dependant upon on our ability...and our willingness...to understand, accept

and resolve an intangible human condition common to all humans: **conflict**. Our behaviors, like our experiences, come from what we learned through the cultural bias built into our social class structure.

All conflict begins from within. When our *Intrapersonal* conflict is allowed to remain unresolved, conflict *will* divide relationships, destroy teams, and separate our best intentions from our best work. After an understanding of the nature of behavior, you will be in a better position to give yourself permission to accept and resolve your own *intra*personal conflicts. Your *inter*personal conflicts, however, are more difficult to resolve as they require the permission of others.

Behaviors to control, both positively and negatively, are second nature and are as common as air and sunshine. We must give permission to be controlled. (Chapter 2)

To resolve your Interpersonal conflicts, there are a few rules to the *Games People Play* to get what you want... and subsequently, some of what you need. The behaviors of children, and their methods of control to get what they want, are much easier to read and understand. We adults first learned our controlling behaviors *as* children. Consequently, children are at a disadvantage as we adults have had much more experience in "playing the game" to get what we want.

To every guy or gal that has ever said, *"I'm not playing their game,"* understand that we are ALL participants in the game, whether we want to be players or not. It is not really *"their game"* that you object to, it is whatever "strategy" they are employing in their "game" to get what they want that bothers you. You can't control the game... but you *can* understand some game strategies. (Chapter 3)

Most people would see an opportunity to resolve conflict as a reasonable decision. As *all behaviors are choices,* however, some people choose not to rejoin relationships and would rather prolong their misery than end it. Misery can be indefinitely extended by simply avoiding productive ways to resolve conflicts. We often tag people who choose not to resolve their conflict as being "unreasonable."

When we carry our unresolved personal conflicts into conversations and meetings, we set ourselves apart from others even before the first word is spoken. When any party in an *inter*personal conflict finds himself steeped in his own unresolved *intra*personal conflicts, personal blame manifests, anger internalizes and hopes for a peaceful resolution diminish. As a result, *inter*personal conflicts are not always resolvable. Chapter 4 is such a story... a story of unresolved conflict . . .with a parent and a school principal.

Those who understand that *all behaviors can change*, seem to have a gift for developing positive Interpersonal relationships. Imagine an elementary school teacher who understood and accepted the differences between human behaviors and human needs. Her gifts as a teacher included a willingness to look past the unwanted, unwelcomed or inappropriate *behaviors* she received from her students. She would choose instead to recognize the *need* that spawned those behaviors. In making a concerted effort to focus not on the behaviors, but on the specific motivation behind those behaviors, she was able to help her students meet their needs. As a direct result of helping her students to meet *their* basic human needs, her students... without even realizing that they were doing it... began treating her differently, more positively, and would, in turn, go out of their way to meet *her* needs. And they would continue to do so for the rest of their lives. (Chapter 5)

In building a culture of understanding, acceptance and change, we begin by understanding that you and I will always require something from each other to get us what we want. We will use whatever strategy our experiences tell us is our best chance of getting it. To prepare for the daily battles of will and control with children, parents and colleagues, begin by arming yourself with an understanding of *The Nature of Behavior*.

Chapter 1

Understanding the Nature of Behavior: The Eight Natural Wonders of the World

"A deep tendency in nature is to become precisely what we imagine ourselves to be."
—Norman Vincent Peale

Earl Nightingale once offered a marvelous little analogy about a couple of farmers and a couple of fields. Each farmer had a field. Each field had an equal amount of nutrients, nitrogen, and other elements necessary for the production of healthy crops. Each fertile field received the same amount of sunshine and water. In one field, seeds of corn were planted: an edible and nutritious crop. In the other was planted seeds of nightshade, a deadly poison. As each field received an equal amount of tending, water, and sunshine, each crop grew to a bountiful harvest: one with corn, the other with poison.

The human mind is exactly like that... what you plant will grow. If you plant positive seeds, only positive seeds will take over your garden. If you plant poison, you need not be surprised that only negativity and doubt will consume your thoughts. Whatever YOU plant will grow, for there will be no room for anything else.

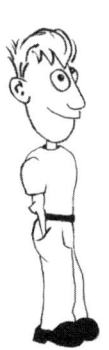

As an administrator in a local university, I remember many occasions when I passed the same young student in the hallway on the way to or from my office. We managed the occasional, "Good morning," but she always seemed so distant, even sad as we hurried past each other. One morning, as she came around the corner, she actually had a big smile on her face, a picture of real happiness. It was so out of place to see even a grin on one so serious, I couldn't hold back. *"WOW! What a great smile,"* I told her. *"It looks great on you!"* I meant it.

From that day forward, whenever I passed that young lady in the hallway, if she weren't already wearing that smile, she would instantly flash one. Her smile sparked my smile. Try it for yourself. The seeds you plant *will* grow!

The Nature of Behavior #1

We humans get along better than we have any right to.

Do you remember a battered and bruised Rodney King when he stood before the cameras a couple of days after the rioting in Los Angeles in 1992? The beating King took at the hands of LA policemen touched off many riots. In an attempt to quell the violence that had taken over the city, Mr. King was brought before a press conference in an attempted call for peace. With cameras running, Mr. King made this now famous plea: *"Can't we all just get along?"*

The answer, Rodney, is YES, but not all at the same time.

What a miracle it is that with over a billion people in this country, we humans really do *"get along"* as well as we do. This is quite a feat, since each of us tends to see the world *only as we want it to be*. That is, we tend to see the *people* in our world only as we *want* them to be— not as they *choose* to be. We operate out of our *own* experiences, so we naturally believe that what we are doing is the right thing to do. If it wasn't the "right" thing to do, we wouldn't do it, right? As a result, we judge ourselves as *nearly perfect* creatures. When others do something contrary to the way we believe they "should" do it; we view them as being everything from suspect to just wrong! Each of us makes this judgment quite naturally as all such judgments come out of our individual and unique world of experiences.

As you learn from your experiences and establish what is right and wrong (for yourself), you see yourself as the model of *"nearly perfect"* (for others). Consequently, since you know what nearly perfect looks like, you expect everyone else to be "nearly perfect," too (defining "nearly perfect" to mean that *they* are doing what *you* think *they* should be doing). Therefore, when others are not "nearly perfect" by your standards, you take it upon yourself to point out to them their imperfections. (Even if you don't say it out loud... you are thinking it.) It is as if it is your purpose on the planet to make sure the *other* guy knows each and every time he fails to measure up to *your* standards! This is not a fault—this is just being human.

After all, when *you* make a mistake, misspell a word, show poor judgment, display bad etiquette, have lousy manners, have a bad hair day, wear clothing in poor taste, mispronounce a word, display a lack of driving skills, etc., isn't there always somebody right there to point it out to you? Maybe this explains why the lady holding the Scales of Justice is wearing a blindfold: We judge ourselves by our intentions...but we judge others by their actions.

THE NATURE OF BEHAVIOR #2

Everyone has an impact on someone.

Robert Fulgrum, in *Everything I Know I Learned in Kindergarten*, referred to that **impact** by what he called the "Fulgrum Effect." He said it's impossible to walk into a room with people in it without dropping something off and picking something up. It may not be seen, tasted, or touched, but the world will never be the same because of it. Whether we are conscious of it or not (and sometimes we are and wish we weren't…), that intangible *something* that is dropped off... and picked up... is the impact we have on others and the impact they leave with us.

Think of a time when you received a warm and generous smile from a stranger, heard a rather moving message from your pastor, enjoyed an exceptional dinner, or received a tender hug from your child. Using any one of a thousand such examples, how often did you acknowledge the impact that moment had on you? If you never spoke the first word about it to the person who had this positive impact on you, how would he or she truly know that such simple expressions of love, recognition, or gratitude meant so much to you?

"So THAT'S why you're like that!"

    A few years ago, while principal of an elementary school, I had to visit the kindergarten classroom to convey a message to the teacher. The teacher was busy with a student so as I walked around the classroom, I noticed a little girl sitting by herself. She was putting together a jigsaw puzzle. While I waited for the teacher, I knelt down beside the child, spoke a few words to her, found a piece or two of the puzzle, and then returned my attention to the now available teacher. My brief visit with this child took no longer than thirty seconds. Had I not run into the child's mother the next evening, I would never have given that brief encounter another thought.

    I saw Mom at a Parent Teacher Organization (PTO) meeting. She stopped me after the meeting and asked me if I *"had a few minutes"* as she wanted to tell me about her daughter. (It had been another twelve-hour day and I was eager to go home. Of course I didn't have a few minutes!) *"Certainly"* I said.

    It seemed that Mom asked her daughter every night before bedtime to describe the best part of her day and the worst part of her day. Mom told me what her daughter had shared with her the night before. She said that the best part of her daughter's day was when *"The principal sat down and talked to me and helped me put together my puzzle."*

    "That meant so much to her," Mom said.

    Talk about conflict…how had I gotten myself so busy that I had forgotten for whom I was working in the first place? Suddenly I wasn't feeling as tired as I had been a few minutes earlier…just smaller.

THE NATURE OF BEHAVIOR #3

A harsh reality: Life is *not*... all about you.

The universal impasse to the building of positive relationships is our refusal to accept this basic understanding of human nature: Life is *not* all about you. Every book you read, every teacher you had, every conversation you took part in, the stories you were told, the playmates you enjoyed, the music you heard, the God you prayed to... *every single experience you have ever had...* has all contributed to making you the unique individual you are. *You are unique; but you are not alone.*

Every minute of every day, every new experience serves only to make you more unique than you were just sixty seconds before. That means that every person you will ever meet is different from you. That doesn't make you right or wrong; better or worse; more deserving or less deserving than your neighbor, the postman, or the teacher down the hall. Relationships are dependent upon the *acceptance* that each of us is different—and that's ok! Imagine that! Our ability to build positive relationships and to see the uniqueness in each individual is dependent upon our willingness to look past ourselves; to reach out to others; to care about what *others* care about.

Each of us brings our own unique gifts and talents into a relationship. The key to *establishing* relationships is in our willingness to look past our differences, to accept what we have in common. The key to *growing* in a relationship is not focusing on how much you are *alike*, but the extent to which you are willing to accept how much you are *different*.

When you first have difficulty accepting the differences of others, you may not realize the changes that begin to come over you. Subtle at first, unspoken attitudes revealed in your inflection and body language can quickly move from internal beliefs to obvious distain. Often without having spoken the first word to each other, you can begin to build walls between yourself and those you see as *different* from you. Rather than building relationships... you build walls that divide and isolate. You will know that you are beginning to accept others when rather than asking *"Who put up this wall?"* you are asking instead, *"How can I tear it down?"*

While it does take two to commit to a relationship, it only takes one person to take the first step. It can begin with *you* placing the focus on *others*. Our ability to build positive relationships is dependent upon our willingness to reach out to others, and to care about what *others* care about. Unfair? You want people to come to you first? You want to sit back and wait for someone to include you? You want others to notice you and then you'll feel welcomed and ready to join in? Well, brace yourself because that is exactly how other people see it, too! If you want to be included, invited, encouraged, and welcomed, then it is *all about you* taking the first step. Be the first to smile, offer a greeting, open a door, shake a hand, or offer a cup of coffiee. These are painless gestures that may literally open a dialogue that may never have had a chance if you did not extend the invitation.

Try this: Pick someone with whom you want a better relationship. It could be your spouse, a co-worker, your neighbor, or your teenager. Got them in mind? Make it a point to meet their need to be affirmed. You can begin by making non-threatening inquiries about *her* (his) interests or hobby, *her* family, *her* work, *her* favorite sport, *her* views on anything from sex, drugs, or rock 'n' roll— anything that gives her a reason to be in this conversation. Everyone is willing to talk about himself, the most important person in his own life. Allow others to feel welcomed and important *first*, and they will, without conscious though, find *you* to be important, too.

Warning! If you haven't done this a in while, particularly with your teenager, do not be discouraged by his/her immediate reaction: *"What's wrong? Or "What did I do this time?"* Actually, they'll be flattered by the unaccustomed attention and secretly hope it never stops.

Try this as an initial step whenever you are preparing to end a conversation. Ask her/him a question, remember her family and send your regards, or leave her with a compliment about something she just shared. In something as basic as this, you are letting her know that you find *her* to be important, and that you *were* listening. You will be amazed at the new "conversationalist" you've become. When you find this simple exercise with one person to be rewarding (and you will), try it out on others. People will line up to be in your presence… with someone *"who really cares about me."* Differences melt away when we are willing to listen (affirm) and accept each other. As a result, others will make themselves available when *you* need to be heard.

To establish a better rapport with teens, teachers, and parents, all of us would do well to remember this thought: *Negativity can not survive in a positive environment.* To be influenced by the uniqueness of each individual you meet, you must become focused on what you have in common, rather than what sets you apart.

I have always admired the relationship that Louie and Teresa Carozza have enjoyed with each other for over sixty years. These are my in-laws, and have been affectionately known as "Gramps" and "Gram" for most of the last thirty years. On the occasion of their 50th wedding anniversary party, I took Mr. Carozza aside and said, "Gramps, I've got to know something. How is it that in fifty years of marriage, you never had a real disagreement? I've certainly never seen one. What have you done to corner the market on marital bliss? What is your secret?"

"Son," he said, "the secret to our marriage is respecting the differences each of us brought into this marriage."

"Wow, that's profound, Gramps. Is that really the secret to your marriage?"

"Well, maybe not completely," he admitted. "You see, every time there is a disagreement, a real difference of opinion, I just remember those three little words."

"Oh," I interrupted. "You mean I love you?"

He smiled, and continued, "No. Every time there is a disagreement, a real difference of opinion, I remember again how important she is to me, I put on my most serious face and offer those three little words: *Oh… Yeah… Right!*"

THE NATURE OF BEHAVIOR #4

If you are not influenced by the uniqueness of *everyone* you meet, you cannot expect *anyone* you meet to be influenced by the uniqueness of any advice you may have to share.

Before you could become a Girl Scout, recite the pledge of allegiance, or even before you could get married; someone stood in front of you and said something like, *"Repeat after me."*

If you are a teacher, repeat after me: *"If I am not influenced by the uniqueness of every student I meet, she (he) will not be influenced by the uniqueness of any advice I might share."*

If you are a teacher, repeat after me: *"If I am not influenced by the uniqueness of every fellow teacher I meet, she (he) will not be influenced by the uniqueness of any advice I might share."*

If you are a teacher, repeat after me: *"If I am not influenced by the uniqueness of every parent I meet, she (he) will not be influenced by the uniqueness of any advice I might share."*

If you are a principal, repeat after me: *"If I am not influenced by the uniqueness of every student (every teacher, every parent) I meet, she (he) will not be influenced by the uniqueness of any advice I might share."*

If you are a parent, repeat after me: *"If I am not influenced by the uniqueness of my child, she (he) will not be influenced by the uniqueness of any advice I might share."*

This "natural wonder" speaks for itself. It may be a cliché, but it is, nonetheless, true: *No one cares how much you know, until they know how much you care.* It is not difficult to do, nor hard to figure out. Sometimes that which is the most obvious is the most difficult to see. One of the more observable ways to demonstrate that you care is to take the time to learn the names of the people you serve, the names of the people who serve you, and the names of people you work with. There are few things more personal or unique to an individual than their personal identity. To get inside your computer, you must know the password. To be invited "inside" the life of another, you must first speak their name. Pronounce it correctly and spell it right.

There is a name for everything...we name everything from horses, pets, toys, cars, boats, and mammals, to every gadget and widget you ever bought, lost or borrowed. We do this to grant each creature or inanimate object its own description or identity. It is perfectly logical, therefore, that parents would labor for months before deciding upon just the right title…the perfect label…that would mark their child with the unique name that would distinguish them as individuals through the next eight or nine decades. Family heritage, tradition, culture, even scripture are often employed to bring meaning to this title. A name is personal.

I had been the principal of a particular elementary school for two years. At the end of that time, the state recognized our school as a "School of Excellence" and I was transferred to work out of the board office. On my first return visit to my former elementary school some two months later, I remember standing at the counter in the front office speaking with the secretary when I felt my leg buckle. I looked down and attached to my right leg was a third grader with a huge smile. "Well, look here," I exclaimed. "It's my little friend SARAH!"

Instantly I felt her death grip releasing from my leg. Her expression shifted to one of those deer-in-the-headlight looks. She almost whispered, "You remembered me." She got up on her toes and stuck her nose over the counter and said to the secretary, "He remembered my name!"

The teacher in the hallway said, "Come on Sarah, time to go."

As she moved to go, she said to the teacher, "He remembered my name." She turned as she exited the door and said, "I love you Mr. Faller."

Repeat after me: *"If I am not influenced by the uniqueness of every student I meet…"*

(An Aside: Though I have no research to base this finding, I would like to state with some certainty that everyone I know on a first name basis *does not* love me.)

A principal friend was going through her class list when I caught the name of a set of twins: Or-an-galo and La'man-galo. The principal, as if reading my mind, said, "I asked the mother how she came up with these names. She told me that after the babies were born, the nurse brought in the birth certificates to complete. Mom glanced to her food tray and the first thing she saw was the menu: *Orange Jell-O or Lemon Jello.*

THE NATURE OF BEHAVIOR #5

Our Behaviors and our Attitudes are not what happens to us, but are the Choices that come out of us.

There is a cycle of behavior that all humans have in common. We select behaviors for the sole purpose of satisfying our basic human needs. Based on what we need (must have), we determine what we want (desire), and then choose a behavior (an action) we think will get it for us. The feedback we receive from our behavior choices will tell us if we got what we wanted. The consequences of our behavior choices (rewards/punishment) tell us just how successful or painful it was. The experiences that follow are stored in our "hard drives" and serve to shape our perceptions and form our expectations for how we think we need to behave in order to get what we want... *next time*. And that cycle will repeat itself every time we choose a new behavior to get something we want.

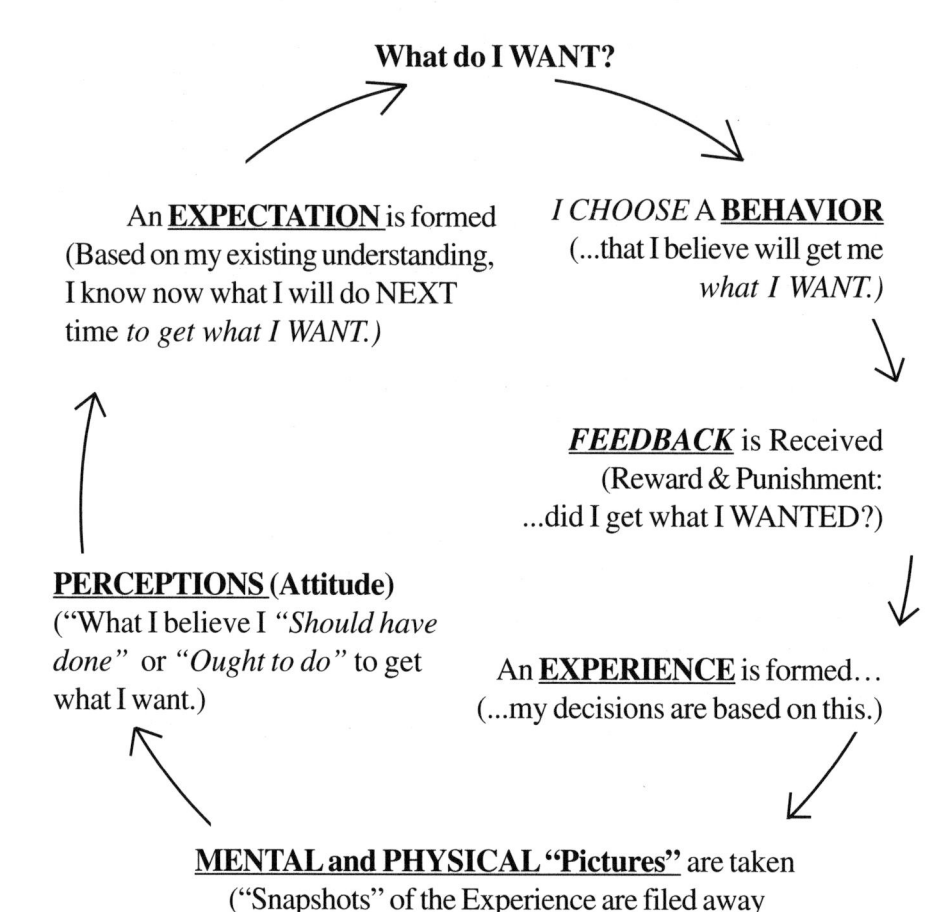

What do I WANT?

An **EXPECTATION** is formed
(Based on my existing understanding, I know now what I will do NEXT time *to get what I WANT.*)

I CHOOSE A **BEHAVIOR**
(...that I believe will get me *what I WANT.*)

FEEDBACK is Received
(Reward & Punishment: ...did I get what I WANTED?)

PERCEPTIONS (Attitude)
("What I believe I *"Should have done"* or *"Ought to do"* to get what I want.)

An **EXPERIENCE** is formed...
(...my decisions are based on this.)

MENTAL and PHYSICAL "Pictures" are taken
("Snapshots" of the Experience are filed away for future reference and immediate recall.)

NOTE: All behaviors are learned—so all behaviors can change.
The cycle by which we CHOOSE Behaviors, however, will NOT change.

This is the Behavior Cycle by which we choose the tens of thousands of behaviors we exhibit every single day. When we refuse to accept "NO" for an answer we select behaviors we believe will control others so they will give us what they didn't want us to have in the first place.

When you ask some people why they act the way they do, the answer may be, *"That's just the way I am."* Such an answer implies a pattern of thinking, or some kind of programming, rather than an understanding that our behaviors are our choices, not our destiny. How easy it is to slip into habits; a pattern of thinking or a cycle of behavior that serves only to suppress independent thought.

All behaviors are learned; All behaviors are choices; All behaviors can change.

THE NATURE OF BEHAVIOR #6

The more we're DIFFERENT, the more we're EXACTLY alike.

Our inability...our unwillingness...to accept the differences between us is the #1 source of our interpersonal conflicts. Our differences are reflected in our choices of behaviors and these choices are as varied and as many as the stars in the sky. Our human needs, however, are few. You can count them on one hand. These needs are what we have in common. *All behaviors serve only to meet our five basic human needs*: Survival; Love and Acceptance; Affirmation and Fulfillment; Fun; and Freedom.

As humans, we have an unquenchable thirst for understanding. We can't get enough. When we don't understand, we fill the void with speculation. When we speculate, we are guessing. Speculation can result in the misunderstandings, misperceptions, and miscommunications that we will inevitably pass back and forth in the form of gossip, every single hour of the day in the search for understanding. Rumors (gossip) may begin as a simple quest for understanding, but left to run rampant, as most organizations will attest, this aimless speculation will divide relationships, destroy teams, and separate our best intentions from our best work.

While the endless display of behaviors (and controlling behaviors) we receive serve only to highlight our differences, take comfort in the fact that we will *always* have the same five human needs in common. To diminish our conflicts with others, all we have to do is to look past the behaviors we receive from others to recognize the need that others are trying to meet. The behaviors which so obviously separate us, therefore, are the very standards we can use to recognize the need(s) that is missing in order to make the relationship whole.

Serve first the needs of others—and you will find that others will go out of their way to meet your needs—guaranteed. (A more complete understanding of this relationship between behaviors and our five universal needs are detailed in the first book in this series: *"So what did you do THAT for?"*)

THE NATURE OF BEHAVIOR #7

The truth is this: All anger comes from within.

Anger does not cause violence. It can, however, serve to jump-start conflict. Students don't throw books across the room when the anticipated grade of A- turns out to be a C+. Nor do teachers bodily pitch students out of their classrooms because kids sometimes know just how to step on their instructor's last nerve. And not every parent is quick to flare and prone to violence just because Susie or Johnny came home with too much homework from school.

We create our own anger. Anger is no one's fault. Outside stimuli can only stir what is already inside us. The experiences, perceptions, and understanding people have within them will "allow" a comment or action to positively or negatively influence their judgments and actions. We can't control what others say or do, and sometimes that "makes us angry." How dare others not have the same feelings, insecurities, or experiences as we do? When others stubbornly refuse to be controlled by us, or they don't see life the way we do, we get "angry" with them and say, "You made me angry." (That makes as much sense as blaming a *calendar* because it gave us Monday!)

Sometimes we could just kick ourselves for the things we say or do — or what we have *failed* to say or do. We mere mortals often have the inability to accept that we could have misspoken, said something inappropriate, out-of-line, or just stupid! We don't always allow ourselves to recover from our own lapses in judgment, to make a mistake, or to be seen as less than perfect. We fear others may think less of us (loss of Acceptance), they will restrict our independence (lack of Freedom), or ridicule our errors, and make folly out of our sincerity (lack of Importance or Fulfillment). We become defensive when we are challenged. We repress an apology and scream when we should have laughed, experience guilt for any one of a number of exposed imperfections, and are quick to point the finger of blame at others *(even though four of our fingers are still pointing back at ourselves)*. Anger is not the fault of others. Our inability to accept our own failings is the source of our anger.

Our repressed feelings become like splinters under our skin; they fester. Because of our own insecurities and unwillingness to apologize, or to excuse ourselves from embarrassment, we become "angry." We don't seem to be honest enough to say, *"Wait a minute, I think I just screwed up here!"* The result is, we direct or project our anger *at* someone. I repeat, anger does not cause violence, but it does increase the pressure or the conflict within us. When unresolved anger is turned inward, doctors first call it Stress. When left to manifest, they will later call it Depression.

THE NATURE OF BEHAVIOR #8

Communications (understanding) is never in the *intent* of the speaker; it is always in the message *received* by the listener.

What we say, what we don't say, and even how we say it—or don't say it—comes out of our own unique world of understanding. Your understanding of the world can only come out of the understanding you have derived from your own experiences. Beyond that, you can only speculate as to the intent of others as they, too, are speaking out of their own world of understanding. When we fail to accept that others have differing experiences than our own, we assume others will understand our intentions.

If, for example, I were to describe a specific event to you, an event that I experienced and you did not, you can certainly realize that you could not hold the same understanding, feelings, or empathy for the event that I would. Even if we went to this event *together*, based on the previously formed experiences, attitudes, and perceptions that each of us brought into the event, we *still* would not come away with exactly the same understanding. (Note how "eye" witnesses at the *same* crime scene seldom report the *same* description of what happened.)

If I don't know or understand exactly what you know or understand (and I can't possibly know *exactly*…), I can only take away from your description (advice, lecture, suggestions, directions, implications, orders, etc.), what my experiences tell me is the intent of your message. Consider this (true) story:

"Coach" is the name even his own kids called him. He wore his whistle to the dinner table, checked his rubber cleats at the door, lived in his practice jersey, and even carried his team roster on a clipboard around the house (…in case a new play inspired him, he wanted to write it down). He was the Coach of the nine-year-old team for the local youth football program. I stood on the sidelines with him during his season opener and heard him repeatedly telling his defensive right tackle, *"Penetrate, Joey, penetrate!"* Several times he felt the need to repeat his urgings to other team members as well.

After the game (they lost by several touchdowns) he put on his best Coach's face, and stepped over to a tired Joey. *"Son,"* he began, *"I told you to penetrate, yet time after time you just stood up! Why wouldn't you penetrate?"*

His little face wrinkled up, and with sincerity, and all the courage he could muster, the boy whispered, *"Coach, what does 'penetrate' mean?"*

The coach assumed that because he knew and understood what he intended… then the boy would understand what he intended, too. Because the *word* "penetrate" was not in the boy's experience (memory, i.e., vocabulary), there was no way the boy could know or comply with the intent of the message. Imagine the conflict that both the boy and the coach were experiencing. The boy could only guess as to what he thought was intended by a word his coach assumed the boy knew. Can conflict begin that innocently? Absolutely.

Conflict Resolution

I recently went to the shopping mall. I rode to the mall with my son Scott. Scott has speakers in the doors, in the trunk, and under the seats of his car. Scott has been building car stereos and alarm systems since he was twelve years old. I love my son. As a young man growing up, the only disagreement we ever had was over our differing taste in music. (He still says he has never heard of Barry Manilow.)

On the way to the mall he tried to be clever and played one of his "tunes" for me. With a big smile (and deliberately poor grammar), he proudly jabbed, *"Hey, Dad, ain't that music BAD?"*

Without hesitation I agreed, *"It SURE is!"* (He got the message.)

As we arrived at the mall, we walked up to the entrance and read this sign on the main door: ***Free ear piercing today.*** We both drew the same mental image and laughed out loud when we saw the sign on the door immediately beside that one that read: ***Archery contest today.*** (It was even more hysterical when two ladies walked up, read the signs, then immediately turned and walked back to the parking lot.)

Communictions is never in the intent of the speaker...

Chapter 2

How to spoil your CHILD and raise an irresponsible ADULT

*"The error we make in child-rearing is when we forget that our role is to raise responsible adults. When the goal becomes "keeping them happy," we are reduced to raising perpetual children.
—"The Stephen Convey Institute"*

Perhaps ENABLING vs. EMPOWERING could have been included in the next chapter under "Games people Play," for this is certainly a "game" that parents and teachers have played many times. In fact, I would say that this "game" is such an ancient and universally played sport, that it is unmatched in popularity for spawning interpersonal conflict. The uniqueness of this game is that we begin this game by being determined *NOT* to play. As a result, I think it deserves a chapter all its own. We enter into this game with the best of intentions.

<u>The Game</u>: ENABLING vs. EMPOWERING
<u>The Rules</u>: The child usually serves first. The adult determines length of play.

<u>A Sample Playing Field:</u> Johnny rushed out of the house after the third "Johnny!" call from mom. She was waiting to take him to ball practice. When the horn blew again, twelve year old Johnny tore himself away from the chat line he was on, stepped over the pile of clothes by the bed, picked up the gym bag and left the room leaving the TV, computer and lights on as he ran.

"Do you have everything?" and "Are you sure?" were the only two questions she could ask before the young one urged her to "Hurry, I'm going to be late!"

As mom returns home after dropping Johnny off at the field, Johnny called from the cell phone he just "had to have" to tell mom that she "has to" come back and bring him the cleats he was supposed to bring to practice. He tells her that his shoes are *"somewhere in my room, maybe under the stereo by the Xbox, or beside my computer, or in the garage behind my four-wheeler or bicycle. I need them or the coach won't let me play in the game Friday."*

<u>The Opening Serve</u>: ***"I need them or the coach won't let me play in the game Friday."***

<u>GAME ON....The Volley:</u> *(It will go something like this :)*
"Johnny, I asked you if you had everything!"
"I thought I did!"
"I asked you twice!"
"I told you, I thought I did."
"When we told you to get ready last night, what did you do?"
"I don't know...I thought they were there. Mom, I just need them *now*."
"You didn't prepare last night and you're not even sure where they are now, so how could you 'thought' you had them?"
"It's not my fault, *you* cleaned them after my last practice, how would I know what you did with them?"
"How about they are YOUR shoes, and YOU were supposed to take care of them. Those are $60 dollars shoes mister."
"Mom, I gotta have them or coach won't let me play Friday!"

<u>Mom's turn up to bat:</u> The next shot could be an ACE for Mom...or a shot way out of bounds. Mom must weigh a few very important options before swinging at this pitch. She will, literally, in just a second or two, determine to swing at a bat pitch, or end the game right here and now.

<u>TIME OUT:</u> Let's put this exchange on pause for a minute to look at Mom's options. Going back and forth in her mind right now... just as these thoughts have passed back and forth in the minds of every parent caught up in the game...are two very distinct, very opposing options.

<u>On one hand:</u> "How will he ever become responsible if I keep giving in to him? I did ask him...twice...if he had everything. Maybe he would be less apt to forget things all the time if he had to accept the consequences for not being prepared. He needs to become responsible for his own actions. This would teach him a lesson if I tell him no."

<u>On the other hand:</u> "I don't want Johnny unhappy. The other children

may make fun of him if he doesn't get to play. It may damage his self esteem if he doesn't play. He may not like me if I don't bring those shoes to him. He'll get upset and yell again. I did pay $60 for those shoes so he needs to get some use out of them. I will be embarrassed in front of the other parents if all the other kids play and Johnny doesn't get to. I would really be embarrassed if he acts out his anger in front of the other parents. He could pout and make my life miserable for weeks. I did clean his shoes, so maybe it is my fault."

<u>TIME IN:</u> *Here comes the pitch...mom swings!*
"Ok sweetie, I'll be there in a few minutes."
"Thanks mom...you're the best!"

<u>GAME OVER</u>...*and the winner is...*
Johnny 1 (one *more* in a series of victories); Mom zero

* * * * * *

ENABLING is a process in which well-meaning parents and teachers allow (even encourage), intentionally or unintentionally...irresponsible and self destructive behavior in their children (students).

Mom bailed Johnny out...again. With a seemingly innocent, *"Ok sweetie...,"* what did mom just *teach* the child? Mother just reinforced with Johnny that he does not have to accept the consequences for his behaviors. Johnny was "taught" that all he has to do is persist in his manipulation and control until mom "gives in." He understands that in the absence of structure, *Johnny is in charge*. The longer the child is *taught* that he will be rescued from his poor behavior choices, his expectations will be that consequences do not apply to him.

If Johnny is not allowed to experience the consequences for his poor choices now...when the penalties are minor...who will the child blame when the consequences for his actions are serious? Will he blame his mom when she can't "fix" things for him anymore? When he fails English Class, will it be because "the teacher is stupid." If he is caught cheating on a test, will it be that the *other* student was cheating off of him? If he is suspended for fighting at school, was it because he was "being picked on?" If not as a child, when will mom stop trying to cover or make excuses for him...and finally allow him to be responsible for his own actions?

In Mom's defense, she loves her child and merely wants the best for him. She simply wants her son to fit her picture of what a son "should be." Unfortunately, she has interrupted this to mean that Johnny should never be unhappy, unaccepted, disappointed, or unsuccessful. As a result, she often bends the rules, blurs the boundaries and threatens consequences but fails to consistently follow through. After all, when he becomes an adult he will never be unhappy, unaccepted, disappointed or unsuccessful...will he? If he is, what will his experiences have prepared him for?

Not always at a conscious level, each time Mom attempts to shelter the child from life's inevitable ups and downs, she is also seeking to be self-fulfilled by his acceptance of her. For when Johnny gets what he wants, mom gets the affirmation she is looking for...and needs, too.

Parents and teachers certainly understand the terms: ENABLING and EMPOWERING. We are keenly conscious of how these play out...*in others*. We have, after all, dedicated years to observing this game in action. We watch the interaction between children and *other* parents, and say we know what we would do "if that were MY kid."

You have been studying child rearing by watching your neighbor's play with their kids. You have watched the interaction between parents and children in the grocery store, at the Mall, at the amusement park, in school, at church, and on and on. You quietly observed all those times when a child stomped his feet at his/her parent's half hearted *"No"* at the child's request for *"more"* or *"one more time"* or *"I want it."* And you shake your head at the almost inevitable *"Oh, ok."* that almost always followed as the 150 pound parent caves to the wrinkled brow of a pouting eight year old.

So what CAN we do to build boundaries in our classrooms and families? How can you establish BOUNDARIES (structure) in your child's life...and have them welcome it? First accept the fact that children not only *want* structure (boundaries) in their life...they will demand it...and they will act out until they get it...guaranteed. You CAN help your children and students understand and accept their obligation to accept the consequences for their own actions.

"So THAT'S why you're like that!"

The Parent/Teachers Guide

YOU establish the Boundaries for your child.
(Classroom or Family Rules)

YOU *teach* (not just *tell*) the Boundaries to your child.

YOU *establish* the Consequences for Behaviors
(both Rewards and Penalties)

Expect the CHILD to push the Boundaries
(Like it or not, the child will choose his/her own behaviors.)

The CHILD must now receive what you promised:
The earned and anticipated consequences of the behaviors.
(Rewards and Penalties)

If YOU fail to provide the promised, earned and anticipated consequences, then WHO moved the Boundaries?

Chapter 3

All Behaviors are Learned: The Games People Play

*"Oh, the gift to give us,
to see ourselves as OTHERS see us."*
—Robert Burns

Remember the days of low budget television? I recall a particularly low budget, unimaginative series called *Lost in Space*. The Robinson family was forever doomed to a fate of fending off Dr. Smith and one creature after another as they struggled, week after week, to bring their lost spacecraft back to earth. As with every other noted outer space drama, this show had a non-human, in this case, a robot, that played a supporting role as one of the mainstays of the story.

This robot had a dry wit but genuine charm. In one particular episode, I remember young Will Robinson was trying to hide from the monster of the week behind a wall decoration that had the appearance of a gigantic Halloween mask. Before eventually facing this demon (it was only an hour show), the robot (imaginatively named "Robot") swiveled, and in that endearing monotone, admonished our hero with, *"You can't hide behind that mask forever, Will Robinson."*

To survive emotionally, you and I have built in sensors, just like that robot. Just like Will Robinson, we recognize that we, too, hide behind masks and that we can't realistically hope to hide behind them forever. The purpose of our masks, of course, is to hide behind defensive walls, to shield our egos, to protect our feelings from a seemingly uncaring world. We also use masks to conceal our attempts to get what we want when others tell us we can't have it. Without the masks, we would have to be blunt and honest all the time. WHOA, who could take that? Pretty soon nobody would talk to us at all.

So, what are some of the masks we wear? What are some of the "games" or strategies we use to get what we want? Choosing behaviors and strategies to get what we want is, after all, the reason why we play these games in the first place. There are many games people play; here are some of them.

Games and Strategies:

1. RESPOND OR REACT

These words are not synonyms. You and I must decide to either REACT or RESPOND to the conflicts that are both within us and around us. When making the decision to either react or respond to a person or situation, these are words that hold incredible significance and emotion. We use these words all the time, but all too often, we use them interchangeably.

If a doctor tells you that you are having a reaction to your medication, you know you're about to break out in hives. If the doctor tells you that you are responding to the medication, you know you're getting better. In the same way, our decisions to either *react* (without thought) or *respond* (as one with a plan) will make all the difference in whether or not we are making decisions for ourselves, or if we are granting permission for others to make decisions for us. We can either react to the behaviors of others, or respond to the needs they are trying to satisfy.

For example, let's say that, for whatever reason, you hate your job. You hate the people you work with, the paperwork, you don't do mornings...whatever. There are three, and only three, intelligent responses you can choose to resolve the conflicts you are experiencing in that job:

· You can *choose* to accept ... even if you do not approve of whatever it is you don't like.

· You can *choose* to work within the system to change whatever it is you do not like.

· Or you can *choose* to quit... just leave that job!

Sorry, but that is it!

Your initial reaction to the last choice was probably, *"You're nuts!"* Or, *"I've got bills, I can't quit."* Or, *"I gotta stay here; I still have mouths to feed and kids to send to college!"* If so, this immediate knee-jerk reaction you just felt came at the suggestion that quitting was one of your viable *response*s.

That's fine. Just realize that your decision— your choice— to remain in a job that you hate, and not to seek a more productive, fulfilling, higher paying, enjoyable, whatever kind of job you *would* like, is still a choice.

You are the only person inside you. So it is you who is choosing to keep repeating the same cycle of non-productive behaviors that will continue to generate this conflict within you. If you don't like your job, you can choose to stop reacting to what you don't like and begin responding (choosing new behaviors), to find happiness in this job... or whatever job you do like.

Many, however, who do not like their jobs, will choose not to respond, only to react. Many fail to see the world as it is...they will choose to see it only as they *want* it to be. They will *choose* to see others only as they *want* them to be. They will fall victim to their persistent pattern of behaviors, reinforce habits through nonproductive choices, stay in those life-draining jobs, and choose to remain miserable. Their ingrained habits often blind them to the realization they are seeing others as the problem and the source of the injustice that is keeping *them* miserable. Rather than actually *doing* something about it, they continue to react to the way *they* think the world is treating them. When standing at the crossroads of change, understand that even your habits are your choices.

Let's say that you really do hate your job. Let's say that the difficulty you face at work, the reason you hate your job is... say... a co-worker; a fellow staff member. A reasonable response to a difference of opinion might be to go directly to that person to resolve misunderstandings or misperceptions. Or you can follow through on the grievance process established by most companies/school systems to resolve conflict. Ultimately, you will *choose* to *respond* in only one of three ways IF you want to resolve this conflict:

1. You will choose to accept—even if you do not approve—of this person's behavior, personality, opinions, or whatever it is you find disagreeable.

2. You will choose to work with this person to change that which you find to be disagreeable, i.e., cooperate, negotiate, assist, understand, etc.

3. Or you will choose to quit...choose to separate from this relationship, this team, this school, this district...this job.

You don't like these options? Then maybe you'll choose a more indirect or non-confrontational approach...and *react*. Let's say that you choose the path that many others have taken before you. Instead of seeking a resolution to your conflict with the person with whom you are *in* conflict, you choose instead to tell other people, *people who can't do a thing about resolving your problem.* You complain to employees, friends, teachers, students, parents, volunteers, visitors to the building, the guy who fills the soda machine, the UPS man, *anybody* with a willing ear.

If this is the tack you take, to react rather than respond, you will be in good company, since many people choose to rationalize their behaviors rather than admit to them. It is always easier to vindicate yourself when you can air your discontent upon people who had no idea of what happened in the first place. It is always easier when those you are in conflict with aren't there to disagree with you. You have the power to make your own decisions! You hold the power to choose a *reaction*...or a *response*.

Imagine walking down the hallway, and coming towards you is a person you don't like. Quickly you react by looking down at your watch, you pretend that something off to the side caught your eye, or anything to avoid "noticing" or having to speak to that person. You even have the fleeting thought of hitting the nearest exit and walking clear around the building rather than having to walk past *her* in this hallway. Amazing, isn't it? You just gave away your power to choose happiness… to *someone you don't even like!*

Now picture yourself driving down the street and someone cuts you off in traffic. You react by speeding up, getting right up there on his bumper, and if he stops in a hurry, you run into his car, become injured, and are cited for the accident! *YEAH*…that'll fix 'em! Now you've just given over your power to choose happiness to someone *you don't even know!*

When you make a simple oversight or mistake on Monday, you often say, *"Oh, well, it's a Monday."* or *"What do you expect for a Monday?"* We actually direct blame on a day of the week and allow a calendar to determine our mood. If someone wakes you in the morning and says *"How are you feeling today?"* What do you say? *"I don't know…quick someone hand me a calendar."* Now you've given up your power to choose happiness to an inanimate object!

Reacting to others and giving other people the power to make your decisions, makes as much sense as allowing a calendar to decide what kind of day you are going to have.

2. "The Bubble Principle"

The Bubble Principle is a concept that allows you to picture yourself living inside this very large, very invisible, protective bubble. Within the security of the bubble is the knowledge that *nothing* can hurt you… physically or emotionally…*without your consent*.

On the way to earning a black belt in karate, students are taught to eliminate distractions. I am quick to tell people that I earned my belts on my knees. For every time I made a mistake, I had to get on my knees…in the "meditation position"…to purge my bubble of the distractions. This was a common practice to teach students their true source of power, patience, and inner peace. For inside, once free from the cluttered thoughts and distractions that were picked up from the world, we could once again fall under the protection of the "bubble." Over time, it not only becomes easier, it becomes a source of great comfort. For only from within will any of us ever truly discover confidence, joy, self-reliance, strength, and peace.

Try it. Wrap yourself in the mindset that within the protection of your bubble, nothing can hurt you… emotionally… without your consent. When the distractions of life mount, hit those knees, and purge your bubble. The confusion and indecision will melt away into clearer, more focused thinking. Do it willingly and often as there are no limits to the number of mistakes you can make or the number of people in your life that seem intent on robbing you of your spirit. The more you are willing to purge, or "let go" of that which you have allowed to seep inside your bubble, the easier it will be to keep it out.

Try this experiment. Go to the toy store and buy one of those .25 cent bottles of bubbles. Keep it on your desk at all times to remind you to visualize the protective "Bubble" that you've now wrapped yourself in. Then, the very next time someone says something to you that may come across as cruel, hurtful or accusatory, allow the words to hit your bubble before you respond (note that you are responding, not reacting). In that split second, ask yourself (and you have to be honest), *"Did I deserve that?"* If so, you have to accept what is yours...and take ownership for it.

If you did not deserve it, choose to respond rather than react. Respond by keeping your "bubble up." Accept that this comment, though it was *directed* at you, is not yours to wear. The instant you have determined that it is not about you, allow the comment to bounce off your bubble and return to its owner. It is amazing... really! You walk away with nothing that you will later have to "let go," and you will feel so much better about yourself. The best part is, each time you do this, it becomes easier to do... the *next* time somebody throws something at you that you don't deserve.

Understanding this concept is especially helpful when you happen to be accompanied by a friend who also understands the "Bubble Principle." When verbally assailed, all you have to do is look over at your friend, smile, and say two words that can become your battle cry: "Bubble Up." You and your friend will both laugh out loud, walk away, and it'll drive your nay sayer crazy!

3. DISTRACT AND DIVIDE

If you still choose to react to your conflict, rather than choosing more appropriate responses, you are about to take your Internal conflict to another level. Venting your anger, frustration, and disappointments on others is a way to avoid having to deal with the problem. It is like saying: *"If I ignore my conflict, maybe it will go away."* Reacting rather than responding is our inability, or stubborn unwillingness, to seek real solutions. We are employing avoidance behaviors when we continue only to hope for, rather than work for, closure to our conflicts. This level calls for us to *distract* (avoid) and *divide* (separate) ourselves from others.

Strategies to distract and divide are evident in your telling and retelling of your "side of the story," your own particular perception of "what happened." It is a well established pattern to garner temporary relief and will, indeed, serve to bring you comfort and support. *But it will only do so for a while.* The objective with this approach seems to be, "I will lift myself up, by putting you (those with whom you are IN conflict) down."

If you persist in distracting behaviors, in doing nothing to actually resolve your conflict, your dissatisfaction will not go away, it will manifest. If your conflict remains unresolved, and if you insist on doing nothing towards choosing more appropriate behaviors, conflict will remain unresolved. Your need to receive greater comfort, satisfaction and validation for your actions…or inactions, will increase. The longer your conflict remains, the more obvious it will become that the gratification you once drew from those reassuring *"what a shame"* and *"poor you"* comments, won't satisfy you anymore.

You had begun to rely on that emotional lift you received each time you put that other person down. Like an addict needing a fix, however, the emotional highs are now harder to obtain, while your need for validation grows stronger. As your friends and associates (do not confuse the two) tire of your complaints, those conscious or unconscious behaviors will serve only to further draw attention to a concern that only *you* are having and only *you* can resolve.

The first law for *how-to-get-out-of-a-hole-you've-dug-yourself-into,* is to throw away the shovel. You are just trying to be validated, of course, for letting yourself feel so rotten. The longer you persist in avoiding a resolution, however, the more miserable you will become and the more difficult it will be to see a resolution to whatever started this conflict in the first place. You don't know how to "feel better," so you trap the next person to come in the break room or the teachers' lounge and recite for him/her your well rehearsed litany of woes. It may not be true that misery loves company, but it is certain that misery will seek out company. So, your objective with these distractions is to hear your colleague say (we'll call him Tom), in so many words, *"You poor thing you; you have been violated! I can't believe that you are being so wronged by his (her) actions! Please accept my understanding and support for your cause."*

If your unproductive behaviors persist, this is where misery can take on a life of its own. The intense energy that you are generating (remember, anger is self-induced), will turn on you…literally. Unresolved anger will turn inwardly into cynicism and depression.

An Aside: Cynicism is the outward sign of a subconscious plea for somebody, anybody, to come to the top of the well you may have thrown yourself into and to offer you a lifeline. Depression is anger turned outside-in. Watch for it. The three most obvious signs are S-L-S: Sad, Listless, Sleepy (the desire to sleep away the emotional exhaustion and escape from the pain).

The longer you persist in avoiding a resolution to your conflict, the more cynical you will become, and the less tolerant your co-workers will become *of you*. People grow weary of hearing that same negative record being played over and over again. Even if they once held you in respect — even if they really do, or at one point did, agree with you — they will soon begin walking away from you when they see you coming. And if others do not agree with you, they will still appear sympathetic because they do not want your caustic tongue gossiping about them.

4. THE RUMOR MILL!

Meanwhile, there is a much bigger picture that you may not be seeing. Your unresolved conflict is negatively impacting the rest of the staff and your school or work community as well. At this point, sides have already formed and the walls of division are highly visible throughout the community. Perhaps you are being blinded by your anger. Maybe you have become so cynical that you don't realize it… or so jaded that you just don't care. But your unfounded rumors and negative comments will not only dramatically influence the perception that others have of you, it can also pull down the morale of everyone around you.

An Aside: There was a marvelous little web site entitled "Rumor Headquarters." The first paragraph of each article it published started with such disclaimers as, *"The following story is false, we made it up. This story is not true, it couldn't possibly be true, and we are stating for the record that it did not happen."* The article would then describe some plausible event that was tied to some current issue in the news. At the end of the article, you could read the surveys that had been conducted and the responses from readers. As high as 40% of the respondents not only would swear it was the truth, many would add their own "evidence" in support of what the very first paragraph admitted was nothing but another blatant attempt from "Rumor Headquarters" to deliberately misrepresent facts.

Acceptance...defined: *The awareness of understanding.*

Understanding...defined: *The internal drive for awareness; to become a part of a group; to seek belonging and meet the human need for peer acceptance.*

Gossip...defined: *A veiled, desperate and often deliberate attempt, in the absence of knowledge, to feint understanding.*

People seldom check out both sides of a story; like lazy, hungry animals, we simply consume whatever it is that is tossed before us. We humans are so gullible, so eager to leap across the chasm that separates the plausible from the *"Darn! How could they?"*

"So THAT'S why you're like that!"

The Behavior Cycle (Chapter 1) reminds us of the fact that once we have had an experience, a mental snapshot of the event or story is taken and placed in the "picture album" of the mind. This is done without our conscious control. It might then take as long as a lifetime to alter that image... regardless of the validity of the information received. It is in this simple premise that we grant gossip and rumor the power to take root. For once we hear or see something, once the experience is etched in the mind... from that instant... it becomes difficult to impossible to shake. The lesson is, if you are the first one to "paint a picture" for someone, to paint your perceptions of reality, then this can become the reality of your listener. Richard Millhouse Nixon probably said it best, *"Perception may not be reality, but perception, for most people, is their reality."*

Take this simple incident as a prime example: Let's say that this morning you made a comment to your colleague Tom when you sat down with him in the teachers' lounge. *"Hey, Tom, got a minute? Can you believe that principal? What a jerk. Do you know that yesterday I overheard him threaten to fire Bill for not turning in that report on time? Can you believe that guy?"*

Tom may or may not have been your friend or ally, but after hearing your comment about Bill, he will do what comes naturally. It may not be malicious, or intended to "hurt" anyone, but Tom's next move will be to rush full speed through the Rumor Mill. With him, he will be carrying his own perceptions... his own version of what he knew and what he heard of the story. Once he filtered what he heard through his own experiences, he will share his perception of what happened to those he meets. It will start innocently enough, by seeing his friend Mary at the morning team meeting. He leans over to her and whispers, *"Mary, did you hear what happened to Bill?"*

Mary will pass Betty in the hall on the way to her classroom and say, *"Did you hear what that mean principal said to poor Bill?"*

Betty will see Henry at lunch and say, *"It's such a shame about Bill, isn't it?"*

Henry will tell Sally at bus duty after school, *"Can you believe it? Bill is going to be fired!"*

Like dust in a windstorm, the many versions of "truth" will spread to all corners of the building and throughout the entire school community. It *can* happen...and happen just that quickly. Once started, it will be impossible to contain, and may have far-reaching implications *for years to come.*

When you walk down the hall, you'll find that sides have been formed and walls built between former friends. Some staff members will offer the principal pats on the back, while other teachers, sympathetic with Bill, are seeking creative ways to drag their feet and withhold their cooperation from the principal to quietly demonstrate their resistance to Bill's "firing."

Bill, the apparent victim, will come out of this looking like some kind of folk hero… and he won't fully understand why. Of course, part of the far-reaching ramifications will be when Bill applies for another job someday. He may never know that he didn't get it because his future employer *"heard"* that he was once fired for some *"unknown reason"* from another position.

And neither Bill nor the principal may ever know that this rumor where the principal "fired Bill" got its start when he was *thanking* Bill for not missing the deadline on that report. He had only told Bill that had that report been late it wouldn't have *"faired well"* for the school. Could someone actually overhear only part of a conversation and leap so quickly to mistaking "faired well" to "fired Bill"? As this is based on a true story... *Ab-so-lutely!*

5. THE "ONE SENTENCE RESPONSE"

We often seek inappropriate ways to resolve the conflict that grows within us. When we initiate or perpetuate gossip and rumors, sometimes we don't recognize that we become a part of the very problem we are fighting against. It can be so consuming, so pervasive, that sometimes we believe we can't do anything to stop it. You may not be able to stop the avalanche in motion, but you can diminish your involvement. You not only can make a difference, you may be able to stop a rumor in its tracks… and still be supportive of the person sharing his (or her) tale of woe…I guarantee it!

Every school or company has one, so imagine walking up to you now is that special someone who you know is about to share with you his or her latest rumor or tale of woe. Remember our previous example? Imagine this person saying the following to you: *"Hey, got a minute? Can you believe that principal? What a jerk! I'm really upset. I overheard him telling Bill that he was going to have him fired for not turning a report in on time. Don't you think the boss is overreacting a bit?"*

He (she) is now waiting for your reaction. He is waiting for your validation and to see where you stand on this issue. It's like a dog that brings you the newspaper. He waits patiently for you to say "Good dog!" So put him on PAUSE for a second or two before answering and ask yourself:

Do I want to perpetuate this or end this? Does this guy (gal) just want to be someone "in-the-know," or is he somehow being hurt in all this and is seeking a confidant? That is, is he coming to me because he wants my acceptance of him and his self-imposed role as the town crier of scandals, or is he seeking direction to resolve some conflict of his own? To know for sure, give him this One Sentence Response…and wait for your answer. With genuine sincerity, respond with:

"So, what did the principal say when you told *him* (her) that?"

Often, a stunned and blank expression will follow your question.

No, it probably wasn't the response he was looking for…but it may well be the response he needed. If he fumbles for an awkward answer, it may be because he had no intention of going to the principal or whoever was the source of his concern or the subject of his rumor. Perhaps he just wanted to be the bearer of gossip to someone who was not as much "in-the-know" as he. If this is the case, you can pretty well count on the fact that he (she) will not be bringing future tales of gossip and woe to you as this clearly was not the hoped for or anticipated response.

On the other hand, he may have found courage in your question and may now choose to take his concern to the source. This is why you must always be sincere with your one sentence questioning response. For when a person IN conflict is truly ready to seek a resolution to his/her distress, your question may be seen as the supportive gesture that you intended. After all, if you were not already involved in the conflict yourself, why else would he choose to involve you? If he didn't want your support what other reason would there be for him to come to *you... someone who can't do a thing about solving his conflict?* Believe it or not, when you offer this response to those who bring you gossip, he/she may later thank you for your guidance. You may have just offered him a way out of this conflict that never occurred to him!

In either case, you have directed him back to the source of his pain or the subject of his rumor. More importantly, you have just removed yourself from being included in an endless cycle of accusations, rumor, and debate. Directing the speaker back to that person with whom they are in conflict is the greatest form of support you can offer. The upside is, you listened, you were supportive, you actually validated the speaker (although not in the conventional manner), you role-modeled what others around you wished they had thought to say, and this conversation is now over.

An Aside: When people persist in talking about you, rather than to you, they are demonstrating their inability or unwillingness to deal directly with their conflict. These individuals are often the source of your office gossip and can be easily identified. William Glasser, the founder of Reality Therapy, put it succinctly into one sentence. He said, *"When people realize that they can't out think, out perform, or control you (to do what they want), they are reduced to only words (in their attempts) to cut you down to size."*

The point is simply this: If you (or the person IN conflict) are not doing something constructive to resolve whatever it is you don't like, unrelenting counter-productive and negative behaviors will serve only to further suppress your joy, create obstacles, eat at your stomach, consume your sick leave, destroy your relationships, and divide your school or work community. Only you put yourself into that emotional well of loneliness and despair, only you can begin the climb out. The longer you remain in that well, the deeper the isolation becomes, the more desperate your screams for help, and the farther away you'll grow from the embrace you long for... and need..

An Aside: We *"silently scream"* for help when we persist in our acting out behaviors, such as chronic complaining, resisting, gossiping, sniping, fighting, etc., *with people who can't do a thing to resolve what's gnawing at us.* These "screams" are our subconscious attempts to draw attention to ourselves. It is our way of getting somebody — anybody, to acknowledge my pain, come to my rescue, validate my behaviors, and somehow do the impossible —*make me happy.*

Ironically, the longer you persist in *silently screaming* for relief with these unproductive behaviors, the more acceptable it seems to be, the more comfortable it becomes, and the more engrained or rooted you become in their use. The first time you hear someone refer to you as "cynical," you'll know that you've arrived.

6. THE RULE OF OPPOSITES

Just listen to those around you who are constantly taking shots at co-workers and the system. When questioned about their behaviors, they speak of themselves as if they were programmed: *"That's just the way I am."* Or, *"I only work here because I have to."* These are the people you will hear complaining the loudest in the hallways and lunch rooms, all the time unwittingly describing themselves in glorious detail to anyone who will stand still long enough to hear their cries: *"Don't they understand? What's wrong with them?"*

The <u>Rule of Opposites</u> applies when people do or say the opposite of what they really want or mean. When we rail at others about their weaknesses or faults, we are often projecting on others what we see (and are upset with) in ourselves. This is another (subconscious) attempt to meet our own needs. Our need to be loved and accepted drives us for this affirmation. Our behaviors say "NO," our Needs say "YES."

This is easily seen in children:

"I hate Bobby." (I really like Bobby.)

"I can't do it; I'm stupid." (Please affirm me; tell me how smart I am.)

"I'm not afraid of anything!" (Except maybe spiders, snakes, scary movies, creaky floors at night, goblins, monsters in my closet...)

"My class pictures are horrible." (I spent hours preparing for this. Please, someone notice how beautiful I am.)

"I failed that test for sure." (You're going to tell me I'm really smart when you find out that I aced that test!)

"I agree with you, but I don't think it will work." ("BUT" always cancels out what immediately preceded it like, "I love you BUT...)

When our insecurities or negative experiences pull us down, we want to believe that others "should" come *to us*—to meet *our needs*, to read *our minds*, to comfort *us*, to make *us* feel better. Rather than expressing how we feel, we do the opposite. When people won't come to us, instead of taking a step toward building the better relationship we really want, we instead take another step backwards. And then we wait.

We seem to actually believe that people *ought to* know through our display of opposite behaviors when we want friendship, acceptance, companionship, and comfort. So we wait some more for others to come to us. We pull back a little farther, frustrate ourselves further, and actually become angry with *others* and physically ill... while we wait some more. We cry, *"What's wrong with people anymore! I've now become withdrawn! I pouted, backed away from social gatherings, and basically stopped being friendly! What more do I have to do to show them (family, co-workers, members of my church, etc.), that I want to be included?"*

Our human need to be accepted is *so* great that we fear that by telling the truth... how we *really* feel... others might not accept us. So our instinct to protect ourselves kicks in. Rather than starting out with the truth, we fish around for hints, compliments, praise, whatever it takes to realize that we won't be rejected when we choose to be more open and honest. And you can appreciate that, can't you? After all, once we step from behind our masks to share the naked truth— and are rejected for it— what else is there?

45

7. SELF-INFLICTED WOUNDS

We choose behaviors that we think will work for us. To that end, we learn through experience what we can "get away with." We know what will succeed, and what might get us more of what we want, and even what won't work for us in the future. Since we base all of our behaviors on our experiences, all behaviors are learned. If all behaviors are learned... then all behaviors can change. We think about it — then we act: We choose to do it, or not to do it!

Even the morning decisions as to what to wear to school or to work, places us in conflict. Conflict is what keeps us up at night. How many of us have difficulty sleeping at night because these "voices" within us won't let us sleep? Because we have grown to associate the word conflict with violence (i.e., pain, suffering, war, disease, pestilence...), most of us have never considered this relentless pull against our will, as self-induced... and therefore, self correcting...internal conflict. We often remain in conflict with our efforts to secure what we need (Survival, Love, Affirmation, Fun, and Freedom) through the choices we make to get us what we want. Acting out to get us what we want (the constant exercise of behaviors, and controlling behaviors, to get what we want from others) can place us in Interpersonal conflict.

So what happens when we think, but don't act?

Jung, Maslow, and Glasser (Book One: *"What did you do THAT for?"*) all agreed that behaviors "begin from within." If our behaviors are our choices, then how can we blame others for the behaviors we choose? We choose behaviors based on what we think. We think, then we DO something...we choose behaviors. At the very first moment that we realize we are choosing *not to act* on what we are thinking, the first seeds of Internal conflict are planted. And we can't blame anyone else for our Internal thoughts since we are the ones who planted them there.

Dr. William Glasser used a marvelous visual to explain this. He said, imagine a car. We have four (4) wheels on this car. Each wheel has a name: Thinking, Doing, Feeling, and Physiology (Physical). The object is to always be in control of your car and not let the car take control of you.

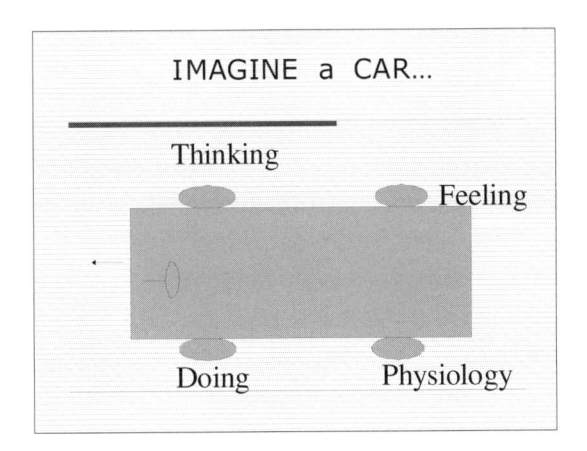

```
              IMAGINE a CAR...

          Thinking
                              Feeling



          Doing          Physiology
```

One of the front wheels of our car is called the **Thinking** wheel. We THINK whether we want to or not. This "wheel" is constantly in motion. Granted, we can redirect our thinking, but the process itself has no off or on button. Think about it…(no pun intended), how many times have you tossed and turned in bed at night, wishing you could sleep, but you couldn't stop thinking? As hard as you tried, you just couldn't get your brain to "turn off" and allow you to rest.

The other front wheel is your DOING wheel. When you DO something about what you are THINKING, you remain in control of your "front-wheel drive" car. When you are in charge, you determine in which direction the car will be steered. But when you are troubled, worried, annoyed, bothered, concerned (or whatever), and you fail to *do* something about what you are thinking, these mental distractions become the seeds of conflict and your power shifts to your back wheels.

When your thoughts are not acted upon; you begin to obsess over what you have no done. Steering is lost as conflict powers one of the "back wheels" of your car…your FEELING wheel. As issues in your mind remain unresolved, you remain unsatisfied, discontented, and confused. You play and replay unresolved events, issues, and conversations over and over in your head. You tell yourself, *"What I should have done was..."* or *"What I should have said was..."* or *"Next time I ought to..."* These will churn in your head and stomach as certainly as a wheel will revolve on a car.

To ignore these thoughts and feelings would be, Freud stated, *"like trying to hold wood under water."* The more you attempt to suppress your thoughts, the more impossible it becomes to keep them hidden beneath the surface.

An Aside: When we bottle up our emotions, rather than doing something about that which is troubling us, we are repressing as feelings the things we are choosing not to act on. Feelings are nature's way of telling us that we are not acting on something—whatever that something is—and it won't go away until we do something. (And you—and only you—know what that something is—don't you?) You can try pretending to the world how cool you are about it, but you can't hide from that little voice inside. There might as well be little loud speakers inside your head, because you can hear those voices screaming at you, loud and clear, can't you? *"Our stomach is killing us! What are you waiting for? If you just keep thinking about it... we'll get an ulcer! You know what's eating at us, don't you? So, DO something about it! Take some action!"*

So let's imagine that you still refuse to do something about the basketful of emotions that is eating at you. That which you first harbored as feelings—that which you once recognized as "unrest" or as a "nagging sensation"—can now take a toll on us physically.

Unexpressed feelings will fester, like a splinter under your skin. Your body has been trying to give you hints that something is wrong. If you haven't heeded the warnings provided by the relentless anxiety, you will now discover what is meant by that phrase, *"So what's eating at you?"* For as long as you choose to ignore your feelings, this is *literally* what will be happening. Your anxiety will shift to your other "back wheel," and your unresolved conflict will start working on your body (physiology) as well as your mind.

When you ignore your feelings (emotions), your body (physiology) will get into the act. From here, you may experience a wide assortment of very real physical ailments: headaches, stomachaches, nausea, inability to concentrate, depression, loss of appetite, or worse. You go to doctors, spend big bucks, take pills, withdraw from co-workers, friends and family, and become miserable. Doctors have a word for all the physical ailments you collect from those feelings that are not acted on... they call it *STRESS*! All the time it was simply your body telling you to do something about what you were thinking as your body now shares an active role in your misery.

You know you have to do something... but what? You've probably already done what most of us do when we are in despair, angry, frustrated, or confused... you share what's troubling you... *with people who can't do a thing about solving the problem!* Like a magic pill, however, the instant you decide to DO what your heart has been telling you all along... to take what has been eating at you *to the person(s) who can do something about your conflict,* you will be rewarded with instant relief.

All you have to do is—step over your pride.

8. THE DIRECT APPROACH

Since "the games people play" will be played with or without your conscious participation, it makes sense you understand some of the ground rules and learn to side step some of the pitfalls. The most direct route to the end of the game is the most certain way through conflict...yet it is often the last path taken.

Many claim that they do not want to "play their game," or they tire of "playing the game." This means they are feeling the very real emotional and physical strain associated with the presence of conflict in their lives. They may be so steeped in their conflict, however, that they no longer see a "face-saving" way out. So for many, before being resigned to a more direct approach, they still cling to the myth that they can avoid it. They prolong the inevitable by persisting to take the option of "phoning a friend."

Let's pretend that we are talking about you... and you are the one who is tired of playing the game. You realize that you *must-get-it-out-of-you* in some manner. But rather than face the source of your pain, seek a resolution to your conflict, or discuss what is troubling you directly with the individual that stands between you and the release of the knot in your stomach, you continue to search for face-saving, back-door approaches that don't exist. Each time you try, you grow more weary (as do your friends and associates) of repeated attempts to dump your anguish on someone... anyone. So why do you persist? Are you still hoping for an easy way out of your conflict? Do you still believe the misnomer that the most direct way through something is to go around it?

A persistent response evoked from our well-intended friends often provides this profound advice — *"Just ignore it!"* (Gee, why didn't you think of that?) That certainly solved the problem, didn't it? (Sorry... that would be sarcasm). You can't walk outside into a thunderstorm and tell yourself to *"Just ignore it!"* You can't go swimming without getting wet. And neither can you resolve conflict by trying to step around it. If your stomach can't *"Just ignore it,"* then you can't *"Just ignore it"* either. It's time for the Direct Approach.

Being direct is not necessarily being blunt. It *is* being honest, even if the one you're sharing with doesn't like what they're hearing. It requires you to step over your pride... regardless of fault... to face your conflict. It is telling someone who *can* do something about the problem.

To do this, you can share what is hurting you. You can ask that girl for a date, you can admit that you messed up, you can offer an apology, you can offer a compliment, you can take a risk, you can do *whatever* your inner voice is telling you to do to *release* the conflict that is inside of you. *It is physically impossible to have a relationship with another if you are not yet prepared to relate to him/her.*

Choosing to be direct in your response to conflict will immediately bring you some level of satisfaction. Even if the other person doesn't like what they are hearing from you, the guilt or anguish you have been holding will no longer be yours to wear. Being direct, sharing the burden of what you know and have imagined over the period that this conflict has been allowed to continue, will release the knot you have been carrying around in your stomach for all this time. In an instant gratification society, this is the most direct path to resolving, or at least diminishing your conflict. And it will occur almost instantly...guaranteed.

Being direct, however, does *not* give you a license to be cruel, lash back, or "get even." If that is your objective, then call it something else. For if your inner voices (and yes, we all have them), are debating with you, and all you are "hearing" is what you are going to say next to hurt, blame, or hide from the truth, you are not yet choosing to be ready to end this. You will know that you are ready to end your conflict, or at least diminish it, *only* when you have given yourself permission to step over your pride—forget "fault" and face the source of your conflict. That is the Direct Approach to internal peace.

An Aside:: My two favorite teachers are Dr. Linda Geronilla, from graduate school, a Psychologist and Reality Therapist, and Sister Nancy Forkort, from the seminary. They never told their students what to think; they taught us how to think. Both taught incredible life lessons. Sister Nancy (who was also a Reality Therapist) helped me to understand the *"voices within."* She helped me to accept that the "voices" could be a comfort rather than a source of anxiety. *Consider looking at it this way,"* she began. *"One voice is simply trying to lead you to good, while the other is trying to lead you astray. When in doubt, instead of struggling with them, separate them. The voice that tells you that you should or ought to do something, may well be telling you what other people want you to do, or what you think others will say that you should or ought to be doing. This voice is the "JUDGE." The only voice left is that of your heart. Follow your heart.*

If choosing to end your conflict, therefore, is what you want, and choosing to be direct and honest is the behavior you've chosen to do this, then above all, remember these words of wisdom from Dr. Geronilla: *"Being direct carries with it a responsibility. You have the right to resolve the conflicts in your life. You have the right to meet your own need...as long as...you do not interfere with the rights of others to meet their own needs. This would place your most sincere and honest intentions, above illegal, immoral and unethical behaviors to get what you want."*

Summary

Think of a time—*really* think of a time—when something was *really* bothering you. (As you think of that time, the actual feelings will come back to remind you what that experience felt like.) The longer it remained unresolved, the more it bothered you, right? Then the Catch 22: the longer it bothered you, the harder it was for you to step over your pride to DO something that would resolve it. And it repeats: You put it off, it bothered you more, the longer you let it go, the more it bothered you...and on and on.

When you finally broke that endless cycle and did something about that knot in your stomach, it was amazing, wasn't it? Once you faced your demon, actually dealt with the conflict you've been agonizing over for weeks, months, even years, the knot in your stomach began to dissolve... almost instantly...didn't it?

You must realize that the knot in your stomach won't go away until you do something about what you're thinking. Take a deep breath... and just do it. Once you get it out of you...it's over! Even if he (she) doesn't like or welcome what you have to say, you just took the knot out of your stomach and put it where it belongs. In doing so, you placed yourself back into the front seat of your car...behind the wheel... and in charge again!

I promise you, once you shift the issue back to your front wheels—by getting rid of what is inside of you—you will have just placed yourself back into the driver's seat. With the steering wheel back in your control, you will once again determine the direction in your life. Rather than allowing yourself to literally be pushed around at will, you will be in control of the most important person in your life... you.

Time to ✓ for Understanding

- Do you now believe you have a better understanding of human nature, of yourself, and at least some idea as to why the people around you choose the behaviors that they do?

- Do you understand that conflict, though unwelcome, comes from within, is natural, and will remain a constant companion? Can you accept that the Internal conflict of others is not your fault or responsibility?

- Do you understand that conflict is the result of miscommunications, misinformation, and misperceptions? And what you meant is seldom what others will hear?.

- Do you understand that you can't *fix* another person? Although you may be well-intentioned and have a desire to be supportive or "helpful," keep in mind that others don't see themselves as *broken!*

- Do you understand that you have the power to shut down the life-draining gossip that whirls around you, and that you can do it in a single sentence?

- Do you understand that you have the power to stop gossip or end it before it begins, by resisting the temptation to *react* to the misinformation, miscommunications, and misperceptions that first come to you by way of rumor?

- Do you understand that when exposed to gossip and rumor the very next words that come from you may set you apart from Interpersonal conflict, or place you in the center of it?

- Do you understand that Acceptance is impossible without Understanding? Understand that people will not change—accept them as they are.

Chapter 4

All Behaviors are Choices: Happiness is Optional

"It is not our Abilities that determine who we are, it is our Choices."
—Professor Dumbledore,
Harry Potter and the Chamber of Secrets

It is not in our human nature to enjoy conflict. In fact, we humans can go to great lengths in our attempts to avoid it. The objective seems to be that if we "ignore it" it will somehow just go away. In truth, the only way to move past conflict… is to go through it. Conflict must be addressed if it is to be resolved. If there is to be hope for resolution in any family, classroom, school, or office, we must first be willing to accept some of the unofficial Correlations of Conflict:

- You and I carry our own baggage, our own internal conflict, into every relationship. It rises with us in the morning and lies down with us at night.

- You and I cannot be responsible for the internal conflict that already exists in others.

- You and I cannot be responsible for the fact that in the absence of what is known, people will choose to fill the void with what they imagine.

- Feelings are not judgments; they are not right and they are not wrong, they just are.

- You and I, while responsible for our own conduct, cannot be responsible for the perception others have of us.

People seek out and thrive on positive and healthy relationships. But when a new experience comes into opposition with a past experience, a number of mental assessments occur in the blink of an eye to lay the groundwork for internal conflict. Being in conflict is as perfectly natural and common as sunshine and water. All conflict begins internally….Albeit, IN conflict. Our internal conflicts are acted out in our Interpersonal conflicts.

Sometimes we learn valuable lessons when we study situations that don't always have happy endings. In fact, learning is present in even the most painful experiences. We must, after all, also take ownership for our conflicts. Sometimes we are left just to take the blame, as blame is far easier to project than fault is to accept. What are we to do when we are at the receiving end of a no-win situation?

Let me tell you a story (well, it's like a story…). Follow me through the tale I'm about to spin (with all the commentary) about a school principal (in the first person), and an angry (though imaginary, of course) parent. The following pages are intended to show the stark reality that not all of the conflicts we face will be resolved or even resolvable.

Your assignment is to note how conflict develops and unfolds and how all the participants involved are (as they often are) in conflict before the first word is spoken between them. This is "real life," as my high school kids would say, except you don't always get to hear what people may be thinking as such incidents occur and are played out in "real life." This is intended to provide an opportunity to accept the nature of conflict without actually being in conflict yourself. So that you aren't expecting some miraculous healing at the end, I'm going to tell you the moral of this story in advance and the hardest lesson to accept: *Conflict can't always be resolved.*

Every story needs a title, so let's call this…

THE *JOYS OF PARENTING*

A school principal wears many hats. As a school administrator, you can be seen as everyone from Father Confessor to Captain Bly. Depending upon the age of the student, the principal (he or she) is seen as a super hero or as the Terminator. Because the teachers don't see him (or her) in their classrooms every day, the principal *obviously* has nothing to do all day. He is seen as a strong advocate for the school or an anchor to the budget of the instructional staff. If a child is happy, the parent can see the principal as the one providing structure. If the child becomes unhappy, as might happen if junior received a low grade, when district policy collides with student behaviors, or when someone's daughter is cut at cheerleader tryouts, the principal is "the villain" and the focal point for blame. To the students in high school, the principal is often seen as the enemy, merely because he/she is an adult. In grade school, the principal may average 20 unsolicited hugs a day.

The principal has no equal in authority in the school building. Consequently, the principal has no peers. So when a worried or upset parent brings his or her concerns into the school, the principal is often the first to catch the ire. The principal speaks on behalf of the staff, in support of his students, and in defense of his school.

When that irate parent believes she (or he) has a legitimate issue to bring to the office (and don't kid yourself, *"build it and they will come,"* has as much to do with schools as it does baseball...), she wants the principal's undivided attention. When the parent believes there is a problem and comes in to address it, almost immediately you can lump those concerns loosely into one of two distinct categories. They will fall under "Simple Misunderstandings," which are the most common and can be peacefully, if not always quickly resolved, or the downright angry, "I'm-ticked-and-I'm-not-going-to-take-it-anymore" (whatever "it" is), category.

In this incident, a collaboration from many such parent conferences, an apparently angry parent is about to enter the school. Note that by entering the conference in the "I'm ticked" mode, the parent is *choosing* to enter this conference by immediately placing herself outside the relationship. Entering this way is like carrying a lightning rod into a thunderstorm. Anger is best employed as a tool to control, manipulate, or intimidate. Remember, the basis of any relationship, discussion, conference, or meeting, be it long term or immediate, is to first *relate* to another.

The Principal's responsibility in entering a meeting or conference that has such a fragile beginning is to make every attempt to first allow the parent(s) to re-enter the relationship. The quest for a common solution must begin on common ground.

So much for background... on with our story:

The principal's office is nineteen steps from the front door of our school. We invite the community in. We literally have an open door to our school and office. Our main hallway is full of life, a warm and welcoming entrance for parents and visitors. On the walls of the hallway, we post our values. Since our values are our people, we display on the left side of the hallway, pictures of every alumni class since the first class in 1958. On the right side we hang pictures of current students. Every time students do something worthy of note, we take their pictures and display them on this Wall of Fame. We also have an Alumni Wall of Fame on that side, along with a proudly posted Honor Roll, and many plaques displaying student achievement. All these help to create a positive culture and welcoming environment for students, faculty, and the community.

Just as McDonald's and Kroger's have their mission statements posted in their places of business, I want everyone to know why we are in business. As you enter our school, above the double doors leading into the main hallway, we have a two-feet by twelve-feet space where the three words we live by are clearly posted: Honor * Scholarship * Service. Hundreds of individuals; students, parents, faculty, alumni, and visitors pass beneath this archway on a daily basis. This is home to our school community.

Parents often refer to themselves as members of "the family." We welcome them into our school and into our classrooms where differences can be minimized and resolved. Sometimes, however, when there is a conflict or a concern that parents believe is severe, rather than bringing it to us to discuss and resolve, they'll stew over it for a while. As we have already learned, INternal conflict won't just fade away... it will grow in size and intensity.

Into our welcoming building now, walking ever so deliberately through the entrance that welcomed her, is one of our moms. I haven't seen her in a while, and she doesn't look happy. Her eyes are glazed over, her lips are tight and turned down, and her steps are deliberate as she heads directly towards me. (Suddenly, I'm glad I haven't seen her in a while.) I invite her into my office (I always do this, as if I had nothing to do all day but wait for visitors to arrive). She has a bone to pick but has waited several days before coming in. She delayed, she said, because *"I wanted to get MY facts straight."*

An Aside: Have you ever noticed how there seems to be a diminishing return on the reliability of facts, the longer you have to wait to hear them? Notice this mom delayed because she wanted to get *her* facts straight. Hmmm...

"So THAT'S why you're like that!"

It never ceases to fascinate me how our detective parents go about getting their *facts*. With the best of intentions toward uncovering "the truth," fact-finding can be doomed from the start if she seeks understanding from other people who also don't know what happened... but they *"heard about it."*

Rumors (gossip) exist in every school or work place. In that search for understanding our minds will stretch to accept almost anything plausible. We hear of an incident or decision that happened without our direct involvement, consent, or approval and filter it against our own perceptions of "truth" to determine the value of the information received. When we then seek understanding, our biases or personal agendas may uncover only those facts relevant to our own interests.

For those who may legitimately be seeking knowledge, it is truly a sight to behold to see how mature, completely stable, intelligent human beings can get so mired in gossip. It is amazing how anyone who claims to "seek understanding" can take something based on the *plausible,* rapidly jump with it to the *it's possible,* then to *probable*, where it is quickly swapped for *it must have*, before they get a running start to leap across that huge *Chasm-of-Conviction* to conclude, *"Darn, how could they?"* For many it is an easy jump, because they choose not to carry any facts with them on their trip.

I believe that there is a direct correlation between speed and duration. The faster it took for someone to leap across that *Chasm-of-Conviction*, the longer she (or he) will stay there — and the less interest she will have in returning. The longer she remains on that side of the Chasm, the harder it will be to convince her to cross back to the land of discussion and reality.

If a person makes the leap without facts, there is a great likelihood that she will be content to use the Chasm as a buffer to protect herself from the facts that remain back in the land of discussion and reality. The longer she remains on that side of the Chasm, she will remain in opposition to the receiving of facts. In fact (no pun intended), the longer she refuses to accept a helping hand to cross back over, the greater the likelihood that she will take root there, holding her preconceived notions and convictions indefinitely. And she will do her best to drag others to that side of the Chasm to share in her misery.

Whatever we mere mortals lack in understanding, we seem to make up for in imagination. In distress, as the mind continues to operate in the absence of knowledge, we further internalize what we choose to believe and whip ourselves into an emotional state. Stack that upon the "support" of other well-intended, yet equally misinformed folks, and a simple misunderstanding can quickly transform a normally rational soul into a conflict waiting to erupt. What might have been a simple misunderstanding has now escalated—*without the first word having been said to someone who could actually do something about the problem.* In this mom's hearing and rehearing of the issue, she is now angry. Now, she wants *ME* to be responsible for what *SHE* heard that made *HER* angry*!?!*

REALITY CHECK #1

When you are about to be blamed for the sins of the world and the faults of the universe, try not to take it personally. Unless you have specific, first-hand involvement in what happened, remember that this is not about YOU. You are, however, the one they've selected to dump it on, remember to "Bubble Up."

Before leaving for school on this fateful morning, Mom's final words to Junior were probably these, *"Now, before I go in there, you're SURE this is what happened, right?"*

REALITY CHECK #2

Mom and Dad, you might want to reconsider this "ultimatum to declare," since it places a now-or-never weight on the child. This leaves precious little "wiggle" room for him to later back out of his conflict. However, if you insist on such a declaration, watch your child's body language with an objective eye, as this is the moment of truth. *Without saying a word,* Junior will immediately be telling you, *"I may have left out a wee bit of the story,"* or *"Yep, I told you everything."*

When this "I'm ticked…" parent came into the school, she came seeking a pound of flesh over an incident at school, a school policy that has *"ruined my child's life,"* or a teacher who *"needs to be fired."* Mind you, the parent may have never spoken with me or anyone else at the school about this concern. Nonetheless, loaded with the child's perception of truth, the child's classmates' versions as pieced together from what she overheard from the backseat of the carpool, and having had those flames fanned by her spouse all night long, she now wants somebody's head. And she is eager to start with mine.

Let's say that the cause of this parent's "outrage" or indignation is the result of some student-to-student dispute. After assuring Mom that she and her child could be absolutely accurate in their assessment, I ask if they can give me some time to check out the "rest of the story," as Paul Harvey would say. While this might be an acceptable and logical first step to dissolving most misunderstandings, this mom again asserts that she already has "her facts" and is now ready for justice to prevail. Roughly interpreted, she wanted to skip the discussion and go right for her pound of flesh.

Meanwhile, my thoughts keep flashing back over several decades of experiences in working with young people. The very heart of the matter for any educator is the reality that we work, every day, with children — immature, insecure, in-constant-need-of-love-and-acceptance — children. When students have a dispute, it can be over and forgotten in minutes. When we more mature adults get involved, these conflicts can linger on indefinitely.

An Aside: The "Golden Rule" in working with children is never doubt that a child is telling the truth. "Truth," however, can often vary dramatically, and in direct proportion to the number of participants (perceptions) involved. The principal's Golden Rule: Thou shalt not assume truth; Thou shalt always investigate. This Mom's Golden Rule: "My child— right or wrong."

I wonder if I should ask Mom if she has considered that Junior may only be able to see one perspective and support just one side of this situation. Did she consider before coming in here that there might be more than one side to this event? Is there more to the story than what she is hearing?

For example, the child may say, *"I wasn't doing anything!"* or *"It wasn't me."* This may be just what the child believes and consequently what perspective (version of truth) the parent holds onto. But is it also possible that the child may have simply overlooked the first four times it happened?

As I listen, I am beginning to form some suspicion as to what may have happened here. I take a risk and ask Mom, *"Could the possibility exist that Junior may have left out just a bit of the story in his retelling of the incident?"*

Yeah, that went over well. She didn't like the *"insinuation"* that her son is a liar. Not having investigated yet, I'm just asking questions here. If the mom is this angry and defensive already, I wonder if the child told Mom the whole story. Why would Junior be afraid to tell Mom what happened? Is his built-in, self-preservation mode kicking in, allowing him to bend the facts just a tad to make sure he wouldn't lose Mom's "Love and Acceptance?"

Did Mom pick up any clues from the child's body language or in his conversation across the dinner table last night? I wonder what she gathered from the child's closing comments as he backed away from the dinner table (and the subject), when he shouted, *"Please, don't say anything!"* I wonder, too, what she thought of her child's parting pleas as he backed all the way out of the topic and down the hall to the sanctuary and safety of his bedroom where he yells, *"Don't worry about it, Mom. Please, I'll deal with it."*

While this may evoke empathy and even anger from the parent, it could be a far cry from what the child may have been saying but Mom wasn't hearing: *"Now that I've shifted the blame off me, let's just drop it, ok?"*

"What a brave child," the parent might say. *"See the way he is willing to burden himself with this injustice?"* Mom's attempt at affirmation will have little impact if the child recognizes that her attempt to support him or emotionally pat him on the back is unfounded. His actions thus far would indicate that he is still exhibiting distracting behaviors and remains, for yet unknown reasons, IN conflict.

Did he fear reprisal from the school? Did he fear a loss of respect from his peers? His parents? His teachers? Did he want it all to just go away? Was he just content that his acting-out, distracting behaviors had successfully diverted her anger from himself? Was his motivation that he simply wanted someone to *listen* to him (to Affirm him), and now Mom is not allowing him (the Freedom) to sort it out for himself? Does he intend to "take care of it" himself? If so, what does that mean? Whatever conflict Junior is carrying, the message to Mom seems to be, *"Don't ask for more details, and I won't have to tell you any more."*

An Aside: Perhaps the greatest affirmation afforded a parent is when his/her child want to share something and asks for his parent to just *"listen to me."* Perhaps the greatest challenge to the parent is to resist the overpowering temptation to do more that just listen. Or did the child also ask for your unsolicited advice, a lecture, punishment, or moralizations? Think about it…be this your own child or one of your students; what you say *right after you were asked "to listen,"* will determine whether he/she may ever ask you to listen again.

REALITY CHECK #3

If Junior got as defensive with Mom, as Mom was with me, flags and flares should have been visible in that home. Even if both parent and child silently agree to their "don't ask, don't tell" alliance, recognize that the anxiety for both will remain. For compromise is not resolution. Therefore, INternal conflict will remain.

I know Junior. He is a pleasant enough child most of time, but the teachers have noted that he can be quick to anger. (As all behaviors are learned, I wonder where he got it? Hmmm…) In the child's protests to "*drop it*," is it possible that he might simply want this to go away because he is having difficulty admitting that he may have had some part in the creation of this problem? Is there validity to the parent's and child's fear that by "telling," the child would be made to suffer? Suffer what… a loss of acceptance? Peer rejection? Consequences for his actions? Is it the school, the student in question, or Mom that he fears? If it really was a concern, why hadn't I heard about this by now from a teacher, another student, or Junior himself?

This mom is using anger as a method of control, almost as if to goad the school to *"take it out on my child; I dare you."* She has determined the "truth" and has now come to see me, prepared to crusade for justice and to defend the honor of her child. She is holding way too much anger for this situation. She has chosen anger to control the outcome; choosing anger rather than reason tells me that understanding is not what she hopes to gain at this conference. Rather than seeking understanding, Mother came prepared only to protect her cub. Love is a strong motivator.

So where did this lady go to secure her "truth?" There is always the usual covey of parents who start lining up an hour before school is out to wait for their children. Add to that the endless hours of bleacher time parents endure in the name of school athletics. Just like people everywhere, parents fill idle time by discussing what they have in common with each other—in this case, their children and their school. And just like people everywhere, in the absence of *understanding*, people will *speculat*e to "conclude" their own version of "truth."

In whatever locations—on the phone, across chat-lines or E-mail—each and every version of the same story is told, retold, expanded, and extrapolated to become the latest interpretation of the last known perceptions... referred to as "facts" of the case. Each version builds on to the next, like the crescendo of a good symphony, to establish "truth." The longer it goes, the farther away we move from common ground and the more difficult it will be for me to provide even some of what she needs (accepted).

So now that the parent has *her* "facts straight," is all in a tizzy and confident that what she has rationalized is fact, she comes to share with me the fruits of her findings. My patience is wearing a little thin as Mom continues to fume. As she drones on, I try to be polite, to meet her need to be heard (affirmed), but my mind drifts. I am amazed at her gullibility. We humans are so eager to swallow a tale; we leap upon juicy gossip and swallow it as completely as a bass would lunge on a worm.

What? Did Mom just say that? She did*!!* She just said, *"I saw Mary at the mall last night* (another parent), *and she heard about it, too, so it must be true."* She actually wants to enter as Exhibit A the "hearsay" from someone else she admits wasn't there and also knows nothing. Oh, boy… this could be a long day…

REALITY CHECK #4

This could be just another amusing paradox if the parent wasn't so eager to hold me—anybody—responsible for what she *wants* to believe. She has her mind made up and I don't think she is going to be distracted with any evidence I might discover to the contrary. I see now why she is leading with anger and doesn't want me to investigate this further. She is afraid that she might find out that what she *thinks* happened isn't exactly what *really* happened. She is going for the knockout, rather than going for a decision. She has already overextended herself *emotionally,* so it will now be difficult, if not impossible, for her to back out of this gracefully.

I allowed her to vent for several minutes (after all, she rehearsed all night). When she reached the height of the colorful picture of injustice that she has been painting for me (and had repeated several times), I asked her *again* for time to check out the story. Surely she is ready to concede by now that I can't "rule" until I am satisfied that everyone involved has been offered the same right to be heard, i.e. listened to (affirmed), as she has.

REALITY CHECK #5

When people are "full of emotion" and need to vent, it would be wise to let them. Keep in mind that you can't pour water into an already full bucket! Always allow the person who is "carrying the most," or, to coin a phrase, who is... "full of it," to be the first to dump some of what she (he) is carrying. If you don't permit her to pour out some of her concerns first, there will be no room in that vessel for anything you may want to add.

As the incident in question occurred many days prior to this mother bringing it to my attention, experience tells me that the actual details of the event will continue to fade farther and farther from memory. In truth, even if I already had some prior knowledge of this parent's concern, by now the story would have taken such a twist that I wouldn't recognize it as the original situation anyway.

Not having the advantage of hearing the many aspects of the parents' version, I now inform Mom that I will take a day or so to confer with the students or teachers who actually were involved. I suggest to Mom that conflict can be reduced and anger soothed when all aspects (not "sides") of the incident can be examined. Mom has already been IN conflict with this issue for days (and nights), so maybe she's weakening as she finally acknowledges my decision to do some "fact finding" of my own. Of course, she can't resist the temptation to tell me that *"it's just a waste of time."*

Her stomach must be tied up in knots by trying to carry all that anger inside. She has chosen the perception that my desire for time to investigate all aspects of the issue was just to *"put her off"* because I *"don't care."* She attempts to justify this conclusion with (my personal favorite), *"I already know for a fact what happened."*

REALITY CHECK #6

Never assume "facts." At least some aspect of everyone's story is probably just that… a story. A story is not a fib, or a fabrication, but may be someone's legitimate perspective on what happened. No matter how many aspects there are in a conflict, all parties can only offer their own version of what they believe… or want to believe happened. That is, they can only offer their own understanding or perception of what happened. Somewhere in the middle of all aspects of a story, there is "truth."

OK, back to our story…

I have taken time and thoroughly interviewed all the parties involved. Mom won't like what I discovered. This is often a delicate time in a parent/principal conference. For when faced with clear evidence contrary to previous assertions, no matter how delicately presented, the one we are hoping to relate to in an Interpersonal conflict must take the next step. That person would hopefully see how she (or he) could have misunderstood, and might even apologize for being presumptuous. The more insecure among us, however, might choose to take a more defensive path and remain in denial of the evidence.

Perhaps she will be embarrassed. Perhaps she will imagine that a staff member or I will see her in a lesser light. In any case, once the facts are presented, whatever step is taken next— to respond or to react— is not mine. Even if I offer my findings in the most affirming way possible (offering her some of what she needs… even if I can't give her everything she wants), only she can choose to accept or reject them: to respond or react to what she hears.

No matter how gently my findings are presented, however, when another person realizes, but won't accept that she has been backing the wrong horse, a red flag goes up when she chooses to remain on the defensive. I know that even if the parent accepts these findings from me, Mom will still remain IN conflict, for she will have a tough time accepting that she has been lied to by her son. (Yeah, that's a good feeling, now realizing that you've been enabling, rather than defending your own child.)

From the posturing behaviors that she has been exhibiting with me, I would be willing to bet that inside her head she is probably hearing something like this: *"If I stay angry, insistent on Junior's innocence, I won't lose face. I won't have to admit that I was wrong."*

"So THAT'S why you're like that!"

REALITY CHECK #7

Always—even if your mother told you there is no such thing as always—*always* be honest with people. Never, ever say anything that you wouldn't want published in the newspaper. You must make every decision as if you were explaining it from the witness stand. If the school or staff is at fault, admit it. Deal with it appropriately and as quickly as possible. When you build a reputation for being honest all the time, you are more apt to be believed by parents (or anyone), when you may someday have to tell them what they don't want to hear.

Well, here it comes. I have to brace myself because the facts do not support her position. This conference could turn ugly, but she must be told. In my experience, if a parent persists in her disbelief, or refuses to accept that her child may not be the fair-headed innocent around his peers that he is at home, there is little I can do to remedy this situation. The result is, I could lose any hope of a relationship with this parent. The choice, unfortunately, to pull-back, to defend against a perceived loss of acceptance, is hers.

It happens. She doesn't like what she is hearing or the evidence that is placed in front of her. Without the validation of the outcome she hoped for, Mom chooses to play the "Should have" and "Ought to" cards. It's predictable and it'll go something like this: *"Well, then, you should have punished the other kid."* Or, *"You ought to fire that teacher."* Or, *"You ought to change the school policy (and make an exception for my child)."* This form of posturing is anticipated and recognized as "face saving." Mom will be able to walk away with at least a moral victory by sharing with others standing outside my front door who are waiting for a report, as to how she *"told that principal what he should have done."*

REALITY CHECK #8

The thought comes to me again. A school principal has the easiest job in the world. E*veryone* is willing to tell him/her how to do it.

In any case, if the conference is too painful to hear, I know it won't be over yet. If Mom becomes so opposed to accepting that her child may have had even partial ownership for the incident, as if by magic, between this conference and the street, the incident will take on a life of its own. Conflict won't just go unresolved; it will explode on the streets. Mom will now have to face all those standing at my door (figuratively speaking, of course), waiting to hear "what happened?" From her preliminary "fact finding," there will be no way her "witnesses" are going to let her avoid reporting back to them the gory details and how she *"told him a thing or two."*

I can count on hearing about it soon, often within hours. She has to regain, in her mind, the self-respect she feels she lost in my office. I will know just how painful it is for the parent by how long it takes for my phone to start ringing. When it does, I'll know that Mom has taken her conflict to the street.

This is when I have to remind myself that the original incident is no longer at issue. This is no longer about resolving conflict. This is no longer about the enabling of Junior. This is not about Mom's attempts to vindicate the child. And this is certainly not about me. She's on a roll now and impossible to reason with. *She has to vindicate herself.*

She was too quick to jump the "Chasm," and she has been there too long now to bring her back safely to the land of "discussion and reality." Trying to stop her escalating attempts at justifying her behaviors now would be like trying to stop waves from splashing against the seashore. While incidents like this are regrettable, it is unrealistic to expect all such Interpersonal conflicts to be resolvable.

It will come back to me that this parent has been making every attempt to save face by telling anyone within ear shot her own version of how this conference went, what a terrible person I am, and how he (that would be me), *"wouldn't do anything about it."*

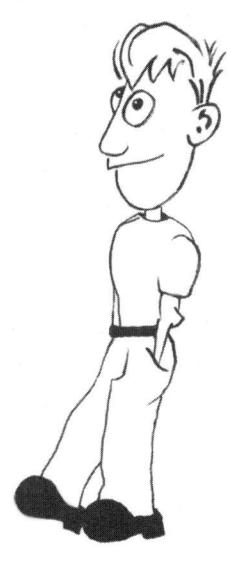

REALITY CHECK #9

It is ironic, but watch your back with people who seek to restore their self-respect. They will do it by trying to discredit someone else. They get away with it by saying to others, *"I'm telling you this in complete confidence."* Believing that you won't be given the opportunity to refute their words, they are now comfortable to amend what actually happened or what was said. They are now "free" to insert their own agendas and to share whatever fantasies they believe will allow themselves to sleep at night; to feel better about what really happened. And because they told others "in confidence," you'll only realize that people you once called friend, won't bother speaking to you anymore… and you may never know why!

If a person remains unsatisfied in meeting the expectation she (he) carried into an Interpersonal conflict, she will remain IN conflict. For many, that means persistently telling and retelling their version of the story (a strategy to distract and divide) out in the community (justifying along with "fact finding"), to anyone who will listen. They seek solace and support that will, in their minds, justify their behaviors. As hard as we want to shake it, the real "truth" cannot be hidden from ourselves. The longer we attempt to hold it down, the deeper the wound becomes. Pain manifests itself emotionally and then physically.

We rationalize that we must separate ourselves from the source of our conflict. As with this parent, she will rationalize that I am the source of her conflict and persist in her agonizing until one of three things happens:

1.) A new cause offers her a temporary escape to psychologically vindicate her previous "loss."

2.) The pain of the wound is permitted to lessen over time (…a very, very long time).

3.) She does something about what is eating at her. For example, she can step over her pride and go to what she perceives to be the "source" (me) of her conflict and be open and honest. (This is the fastest and most direct route to eliminating the knot in her stomach and placing herself back behind the wheel of her car.)

When conflict remains unresolved, people who stubbornly choose (and we do choose) to remain IN conflict tend to justify destructive behaviors rather than apologize for them. When we believe we have been "wronged" by another, and the conflict remains unresolved, we tend to lift ourselves up by verbally putting others down. That way, *"When I bring you down to my level, I make you miserable, just as miserable as (I imagined) you made me. And this makes* me *happy again."*

REALITY CHECK #10

Have you ever noticed that the longer a break in a relationship remains, the harder it will be for the relationship to heal? Freud said it best (and it bears repeating): Even though we try to pretend that being IN conflict doesn't bother us, INternal conflict doesn't go away, we harbor it. *"Attempting to hold in our experiences is like trying to hold wood under water,"* he said. *"Sooner or later, it must rise to the surface."* Because we won't let it go, admit a failing, dismiss guilt, or face our demon, we take that which so deeply troubles us and actually grant ourselves permission for conflict to take root.

If we don't take control of our own conflict, taking action to release the internal thoughts that trouble us, we can become prisoners in our own bodies. Our feelings will then consume us, further altering our Interpersonal relationships and negatively impacting our emotional and physical health. The longer we follow the advice of those who say *"just ignore it,"* unresolved INternal conflict will manifest itself outwardly, like wood that can't forever be held under water. Headaches, stomachaches, nausea, backaches, and other physical pain will persist as not-so-gentle reminders that something is drastically wrong.

All of life is awareness. Yet we remain unaware. Even as these signs continue to warn us, we still try to ignore that which even our bodies are *pleading* with us to remember. The more we try to hide or repress our conflict (feelings), the more we can count on it being revealed through our *Words, Inflection and Body Language.* (Book 3 in this series.)

Epilogue

Stopping short of physical violence, I have tried to paint with this story a "worst case" depiction as to how Interpersonal conflict might begin, through no fault of your own, and how, regardless of your best efforts, conflict may remain unresolved and relationships irrevocably lost. Rejection can be traumatic, even debilitating, regardless of your best attempts to resolve the conflict.

While this mom will continue to actively vent on this issue for a few more weeks, the more unfortunate result may be the permanent loss of relationship with the larger school community and me. Not just with this mom, but with everyone. This mom has contacted to spread her seeds of mistrust. She will not likely let up until her personal need for vindication has been reached. Having now spread "face-saving" untruths in the community to justify her actions, she will have succeeded only in escalating conflict. For as long as she chooses to ignore the INternal conflict she is harboring, she will undoubtedly go out of her way to avoid me, other school personnel, and even other parents who remain supportive of the school. We do that as humans as self-protection for our bruised feelings and egos.

While such parent/principal conferences as I've just described are rare, this is an example of conflict that will not be resolved. Conflict will be inevitable whenever one or more people, holding one or more separate "pictures" (experiences), refuse to acknowledge that their "picture" is not the only "picture." The unwillingness of just one person in an Interpersonal conflict to peacefully work to resolve differences will destroy relationships. Sadly, seldom will it destroy only one relationship.

We've all been there. Intellectually you *know* that you can't be responsible for the experiences, perceptions, or attitudes another person will bring to a conversation with you. And you know that you can't fix people. You can only speak with others, listen to them, understand and accept them. Don't wear what isn't yours to wear. You can't control or fix anybody else in this world but you (though that doesn't seem to stop us from trying...). Therefore, you can't control the conflict that rages in others... only within yourself.

We can, however, still work to minimize and resolve conflict in ourselves. This is a mandatory step in preparing ourselves to meet the needs of others. The goal is to minimize and resolve our own conflicts, in order to assist in the resolution of Interpersonal conflicts with others. The lesson is, unless both parties are willing to understand conflict and accept their mutual responsibility for the resolution of conflict, then not ALL conflicts will be resolved.

Chapter 5

All Behaviors can Change: The Application of Understanding

*"In the end, we will LOVE
only what (and who) we UNDERSTAND.
We will understand, only what we KNOW.
We will know only what we are TAUGHT."*
—Chinese Proverb

It was nearly twenty years ago, but I still remember an article I read that was written by the late syndicated columnist, Sydney Harris. He was relating an incident he and his friend had at a local newspaper stand and it went something like this: He said he and his friend walked up to the paper stand where they patiently waited for service. Finally, as they were approached by the attendant, they were addressed in almost an accusatory tone, *"What do ya' want?"*

The man with Sydney Harris pleasantly responded, *"I would like to have a copy of the London Times, please."*

"Just a minute," came the abrupt response. The man returned a minute later, slapped the paper on the counter and snapped, *"That's six bits."* The friend offered the money to the attendant and received a cold, *"Hold on,"* as he turned to make change. Another moment or two later, the attendant returned, and slid the change across the counter without a word.

"Thank you," the friend directed to the man who had already turned around and moved away. He recovered his change from the counter and turned to leave. As Sydney Harris and his friend moved away from the stand, Sydney stopped his friend and questioned, *"Wait a minute, I've got to know something. Do you come here everyday for a newspaper?"*

"Yes," replied his surprised friend. "Everyday. Why?"

"I have got to know something; does that man treat you like that everyday?"

"Yes," his friend answered, "I'm afraid he does."

"Then now I really need to know, how can you take that? He was just rude and hateful, and you even said, 'Thank you' for that!? Doesn't the way he treats you make you angry?"

The friend was surprised, as if the thought never crossed his mind, but he stared at his friend as if the answer was obvious. His response was classic, and the perfect validation of the fact that all behaviors are choices that come from within. *"We all make our choices in life."* he responded. *"So I don't want **him** to decide what kind of day **I'm** going to have."*

* * * * *

Once upon a time, there was a young school teacher who had a gift for being able to *understand, accept, and resolve* Interpersonal conflict. She knew the basics. She understood that all people come from their own unique and different world of experiences. She knew that all people are simply doing the best they can for what they know and understand. She accepted that because behaviors and perceptions were based on each person's unique experiences, then all people would naturally hold different perceptions, levels of knowledge, and degrees of understanding. She would not assume that people were acting in an unnatural way merely because their choices in behaviors differed from her own.

Even for one so young teacher knew that all people made choices based on their own understanding of the world to that moment in their lives; an understanding that came through their unique experiences, perceptions, and attitudes. She knew that when people didn't at first get what they wanted, they would attempt to control to get what they wanted. She understood the difference between behaviors and needs (see Behavior Cycle). She knew that All Behaviors are Learned; All Behaviors are Choices; All Behaviors can Change.

She accepted that happiness was a choice we all make for ourselves. She had accepted that people do not, as a rule, choose to be hateful, mean, unkind, or offensive to others merely for the express purpose of being hateful, mean, unkind, or offensive to others. She accepted that beyond every behavior she had ever witnessed on this planet, there was a human need that motivated that behavior.

Through her patience, willingness, and commitment to looking past her own immediate wants she learned she could better recognize the missing needs in others. With practice, she learned that she could develop the gift of looking past negative behaviors to recognize what need motivated the behavior. In doing so, she knew she would be able to help others get some of what they needed. (The *survival* need; the need for l*ove and acceptance*; the need to be *fulfilled, affirmed and really listened to;* the need for f*un*; the need for the *freedom to make creative, responsible decisions* for ourselves.) And she accepted the fact that when she worked to meet the needs of others, then others would in turn go out of their way to meet her needs—and they would do it eagerly and without even realizing they were doing it!

This caring young school teacher had developed a gift for entering the world of others. Armed with an understanding of how we choose behaviors and an acceptance that our basic needs are why we choose behaviors, she knew that she possessed the tools to resolve conflict. She was convinced that any success she might have in reaching and teaching children would be in direct proportion to the degree by which she could assist children in resolving their conflicts… and she could prove it.

* * * * *

She had just moved into the area and had accepted a position in a nearby school district to teach in a rural elementary school. She would be the sixth teacher in this particular fifth grade class classroom *that year* - and it was only January. At the time of her hiring, of course, she wasn't aware that so many teachers *had already* been assigned to this class… and had subsequently walked out. This didn't count the many substitute teachers that had been called in to "contain this class between teachers." (A phrase later used by the Assistant Superintendent in the retelling of this story.)

The other teachers in the building saw so many other teachers come and go before her, they didn't even bother to learn her name. They were so sure that she would not last that they referred to her only as **"The Teacher down the Hall."**

"So THAT'S why you're like that!"

When she arrived at the school, this was her immediate first impression: *"I can still see it: The school was dirty, the mood was dark, and the walls barren of all forms of student achievement. Yet all that was going through my mind was, this is the last day I'll be wearing heels."* Her classroom was literally all the way at the end of that long, dreary hallway. Once into her room, she was struck by the similarities between the school and the classroom: *"The classroom was dirty, the mood was dark, and the walls barren of all forms of student achievement."*

As the students filed in on her first day, it didn't take long to realize that this class clearly saw themselves "in charge." They were eager to provide her with the litany of teachers who had come and gone before her.

She was quick to point out that these children were not violent, mean, or even disrespectful. They were controlling, immature, and in desperate need of structure in their day. But this was not to be unexpected. The twenty-four fifth graders in this classroom had literally been, by omission, taught that in the absence of structure (boundaries), chaos reigns! They had learned that the absence of consistent boundaries provided the implied consent to continue with what worked for them in the past.

Their experiences over the previous few months, confirmed by the feedback they had been receiving, reinforced their negative attitude towards school, learning, and *new* teachers. Their learned behaviors had become habits formed over many months and were now deeply engrained. While understanding that habits are hard to break, she accepted that all behaviors are learned... *so All behaviors could change*. And she was up to the challenge.

It began when she realized that the children had copied all the answers from the teacher's manuals into their student workbooks. She bought three boxes of those huge gummy erasers and spent her first week of school reestablishing structure. She directed her new students in the erasure of all notes and information written in their workbooks and textbooks (not to mention desktops, lockers, and walls).

She remembered the "Rule of Opposites," realizing that people will act one way, but mean something totally different. Each time the students got rowdy, and "acted out," she would reassure them with, *"I love you; I'm not going to leave you."* Their behaviors were saying, *"That's what the others said, too.* But their needs were saying, *"Prove it to us... Please!"*

They were exhibiting behaviors that were in direct opposition to their need for love, belonging, and acceptance. One teacher after another, including the other teachers in the building, had few nice things to say either about them or to them. Because others had focused on their behaviors, and not on their needs, these were children who had come to believe that they were neither loved nor loveable. How true the phrase; "The children who are the hardest to love, need love the most."

Her education taught her the basic tenant of behavior management: *"You must acknowledge the behaviors that you want repeated."* So she caught them when they demonstrated positive behaviors and acknowledged them for it. She often reminded these children that she loved them... and she meant it. It wasn't just in her words, for her inflection and body language affirmed it.

Having had a lot of practice behaving as a group, the class was very good at displaying controlling behaviors as a group. One day, as she was writing on the blackboard, each student in the class had conspired to take his or her textbooks and deliberately let them slide off of their desks in unison onto the concrete floor… BANG! Startled, she quickly turned around. It took no more than a moment for her to see what had happened. She would have only another moment to either *react or respond* to their behaviors. (What would you have done?)

In their faces and suppressed laughter, she could see that they were waiting to see how their challenge was going to be answered. In that moment, she stepped over to her own desk, took a pile of her own books, eased them to the edge, then deliberately slid them onto the concrete floor… BANG! *"Sorry I was late,"* she said, *"I'll do better next time."* She smiled, she passed the test, and continued with the lesson.

On another occasion, a very large boy, one who could have passed for a high school varsity football player instead of a fifth grader, had been strangely and uncharacteristically quiet all day. She described him as an "atypical bully." He always wanted the other kids to know how tough he was, but he was never really cruel or mean to them.

As the students were leaving for recess one morning, she could see he was getting angry over something as he suddenly approached her. He started yelling about a poor grade he had received, grabbed her under the arms, and physically lifted her off the ground and against the wall. She remembered being stunned by his actions, yet, she said, never really feeling threatened by him.

The "grade" he had just received before recess could not have been the problem since he had been withdrawn all day. She remembered his pride and said, *"Wow, how strong you are! Your parents must be so proud of you. Please, put me down now, and I'll listen to you."*

Immediately embarrassed, ashamed by his sudden display and prepared for his immediate ejection from the room, and from the school, he lowered her gently and started for the door. She reached for him, and the big bulk of a boy winced as if expecting to be beaten. Instead, looking past his behavior, in front of the other children still in the room, she hugged him. She then led him to a chair.

"Johnny," she began, *"next time, if you want my attention… if you want my help… all you have to do is ask, and I promise, I'll listen to you."* As he cried and shared, she (Affirmed) *listened to him.* After that day, it never took much more than a nod in his direction to get his complete attention. She already had his complete respect.

One particular little boy in this classroom had accumulated a great deal of absences. He didn't seem to be sick or sickly, he just didn't like school… so he stayed home and helped out on the farm. It was not uncommon for him to miss one or two days every week. Consequently, his grades were terrible and well on their way to miserable. She remembered him as being an exceptionally quiet child and secretly thought of him as *"the boy without a smile."* His family was not well off, his clothes were dirty, well-worn, and often in need of stitching. The work boots he wore were always filthy and in dire need of repair.

She told him that her son was about his size and had some extra clothes he didn't wear. She asked him if he would mind wearing them. She also said her husband had a pair of boots that were too small for him. She wondered if he would *"do her a favor"* and get some use out of those boots since her husband wouldn't wear them anymore. He said, *"Yes."*

That night she picked up some of "her son's clothes" and bought a new pair of "her husband's boots" from K-Mart. The next day she gave them to the boy. The boy was delighted. The family, on the other hand, took offense to what they perceived as "charity." It was strange, really, because the family didn't object to the new jeans he was given, they only objected to the new boots (although she didn't know this until years later). Even though his dad refused to let him have the boots, apparently the boy had decided to keep and wear them.

He just never took them home and he never told anyone at school that he wasn't permitted to keep them.

It seemed that the boy was so pleased to receive these new boots from his teacher that every evening after school he would put his new boots in a bag and hide them under his bus stop. Every day on his way to school, he ducked into the bus stop, take his old boots off, put them inside the bag, then put on his new boots for school. He would then put the old boots under the bus stop until after school when he performed that same ritual in reverse. At school, the boy was very proud to be sporting new jeans and new boots. It allowed him to feel better about himself and granted him the self-confidence to begin the establishment of a better rapport with his peers. From the day he first wore those new jeans and boots to school, he missed only three days of school the rest of the year.

Because he was in school, and wanted to be in school, he was able to, and wanted to, keep up academically with the other kids. With his attendance no longer an issue, his grades improved, and his self-respect was restored—so was his smile.

For several children in this rural setting, the free lunch they received each day was the last full meal they would have until the free breakfast they received the next morning. After lunch, any unopened milk, or uneaten fruit would be marked and plastic bags provided for those who wanted to save their treats or biscuits. The children could place these in the used refrigerator the teacher had purchased and kept in the corner of her room.

After school, for all those kids who had to wait for that long bus ride home each night, she waited with them. She opened that refrigerator, and performed a multiplication of the loaves. She pulled out their left over milk and fruit, plus sandwiches, juice, cookies, treats, and other goodies out of that old refrigerator that never seemed to go empty. Not one parent ever objected…

It has been decades now since this particular young teacher taught in that rural school. Yet these "kids," now adults with children of their own, *still* seek her out. She kept her word to "her kids," as these fifth graders referred to themselves, when she promised, *"I won't leave you."*

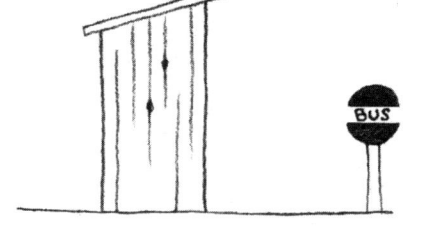

They knew that others referred to her as "The Teacher Down the Hall," so it seems that they have affectionately kept that title for her. They greet her at the mall, stop her at the grocery store, or knock on our front door to speak with her—my wife, Irene—and still call her "*The* Teacher." They bring their children to introduce them, with great pride, to *Their* Teacher. They would ask her to *"talk to my kid like you talked to me."*

She met the needs of her students. In return, they go out of their way to meet her needs...(for acceptance and belonging) *and they are not even aware they are doing it.* While they certainly appreciated the impact Irene had on their lives, these young people are not bartering for her affection, as one might barter services in lieu of currency. Neither are they attempting to "buy" her favor by attempting to exchange acts of kindness, as if what they received from her was a tangible debt that needed to be repaid. Instead, the expressions of kindness, affection, and respect that continue to be returned to her after all these years are an inherent response to her deliberate and unselfish efforts to simply meet their basic human needs. From virtually her first contact with these students, they had been treating her differently (than any other teacher they ever met), more positively, and they didn't even realize why they were doing it. She simply made the conscious effort to look beyond the behavior to help them meet their needs.

As young people, and now as adults, these young men and women are giving back to her a measure of what they received. Her student's lifelong behaviors to meet her need for Acceptance and Affirmation are testimony to the impact one human can have on another — when one solitary life is willing to work to resolve the conflict in others. They have, and will continue to, treat her with love and respect. It is their unspoken and subconscious way of saying *"Thank You."* It is their way of saying, *"We love you, too, and We won't leave You."*

The Moral of the Story?

Life is not...all about **You**! However, only *You* can be responsible for *You*. Only you can choose your behaviors. Only you can choose to remain in an emotional well—the well cannot choose you. You can choose to serve only you, or you can choose behaviors that will serve others; behaviors that will also reward you! Work to resolve the conflict in others, and expressions of admiration, gratitude, love, and respect will follow you. It is as certain and as natural as sunshine: First seek to meet the needs of others, and others will trip over themselves to meet your needs... Guaranteed!

"So THAT'S why you're like that!"

A final thought...

You want a better life. You want the conflict(s) to stop. You want better relationships with those around you. You want people to like you, to respect you, and to include you in their lives. You want a life full of fun, family, and friends. You want to stop *hoping* for it... and begin realizing it. Then it is—as it has always been—all about YOU to make that happen. Begin now. Life is *not* a dress rehearsal.

The behaviors you have chosen in this life have been your best attempts, for what you knew (fact) and understood (perceived), to meet your Needs (five Basic Needs). All of your behaviors were motivated by your *Need to Survive, be Loved and Accepted, Affirmed and Fulfilled,* and to find *Fun and Freedom* in your life. While each person seeks different behaviors to meet their Needs, all choose behaviors for this same reason. In your attempts to seek behaviors to meet *your* NEEDS, you have based those decisions on your past experiences; experiences that have "worked for you." In doing so, you have been building behavior habits. Slowly, over a period of time, and without even realizing it was happening, many day to day conscious decisions were being replaced by subconscious habits. Your habits were becoming so comfortable that it just became easier to follow *"the way I've always done it."* Now, to step out of from behind those habits, you have only to give yourself permission.

If you choose to do something different than yesterday...that choice belongs to you...and you alone. You will have the opportunity to make new decisions some 50,000 times a day...everyday. Even the decision *not* to decide...is yours. To believe that you *"have to"* do something, such as stay in a repressive relationship, remain in a job you hate, withhold a compliment, ask for a raise, or keep gaining weight because you just "have to have" another donut, are simply habits you have fallen into.

Your desire to find happiness, more appropriate relationships, a better job, or to do whatever you believe will bring you peace from the conflict(s) within...is as close to you as the very next decision you make. It has not been your *destiny*, but your *decisions* that have led you to this point in your life. Not happy with the habits that have taken you here? Then make a plan, abandon your habits, and take the first step in a direction that only YOU can decide.

Peace,

Human Resource Leadership Consultants

Serving business and educations most essential assets

Presents

Motivation - Leadership - Communiciation
Books * Seminars * Keynote Presentations
It's ALL About YOU!
"What did you do THAT for?"
"So THAT'S why you're like that!"
Coping with Conflict
Understanding Words - Inflection - Body Language
Mastering the Art of Listening

TOD FALLER has been a national presenter, providing Communication, Leadership, and Motivation seminars, from Green Bay to Jacksonville, since 1986. "The Teacher Down the Hall" Seminar Series provides conflict resolution solutions through an understanding and acceptance of the nature of our Human Behavior. All seminars are fast paced, "user friendly," and GUARANTEED!

If you have questions, would like further information, or would like Mr. Faller to speak with your school, business or organization, please contact us at:

Human Resource Leadership Consultants
3005 Brierwood Rd., Culloden, WV 25510
www.todfaller.com
email: tod@todfaller.com

Headline Books & Co.

P. O. Box 52
Terra Alta, WV 26764
800-570-5951 www.headlinebooks.com